# A MILLION STEPS

## DISCOVERING THE LEBANON MOUNTAIN TRAIL

I dedicate this book to my father, Said El-Hibri, and our dear friend, John Ewing. Both, for different reasons, are not with me today.

Winner of the "Certificate of Merit" for
best art book at the Premier Print Awards 2010

It is not because things are difficult that we do not dare;
it is because we do not dare that things are difficult

*Lucius Annaeus Seneca* (5BC – 65AD)

First published in 2011 by

INTERLINK BOOKS
An imprint of Interlink Publishing Group, Inc.
46 Crosby Street, Northampton, Massachusetts 01060
www.interlinkbooks.com

Designed by Catherine Cattaruzza

Library of Congress Cataloging-in-Publication Data available
ISBN 978-1-56656-839-5

*A portion of the proceeds from the sale of this book will be donated
to the Lebanon Mountain Trail (LMT) Association.*

Printed in Lebanon by 53 Dots (Dar el-Kotob).
Bounded Fouad Baayno Bookbindery sarl.

To request our complete 48-page full-color catalog, please call us toll
free at 1-800-238-LINK, visit our website at www.interlinkbooks.com,
or send us an e-mail: info@interlinkbooks.com

# A MILLION STEPS

## DISCOVERING THE LEBANON MOUNTAIN TRAIL

HANA EL-HIBRI
PHOTOGRAPHS BY NORBERT SCHILLER
FOREWORD BY MAXIME CHAYA

INTERLINK BOOKS
An imprint of Interlink Publishing Group, Inc.
Northampton, Massachusetts

# Thanks

**To my husband** Bassem for his support and encouragement; to my son Hatim for his insights and unwavering belief in my ability, Belal's artistic input and 'tech support' and Hadi for adapting to mom's unusually busy schedule; to my mother, Hind; my brother, Anas and my sister, Arwa; to Maurice and Nicholas Sehnaoui; to the staff at DOTS, in particular Wael Jamaleddine, Youssef Joujou and Mazen Hasbini; to Catherine Cattaruzza with whom it was a pleasure to collaborate and who instinctively knew what I wanted; to the staff at ECODIT, especially Faisal Abu Izzeddine, Karim El-Jisr and Joyce Jadam, who made all their resources available to me, fact checked the text and generously sponsored Norbert and I on the thru-walk; to all our guides, each of whom shared with us their special part of the mountains.

To Charlotte Hamaoui, whose friendship and advice helped guide me through the tribulations and complexities of publishing a book and to her team at Turning Point: Eleena Sarkissian, Nadine Hatem and Nasrin Aboulhosn; to Joseph Karam for his vision; to my wonderful editor Michael Karam whose judgment and advice were invaluable in making my message come out perfectly; to the LMT Association, in particular Pascal Abdullah, John Kairouz, Christian Akhrass and Nizar Hani; to Michel Moufarege who introduced me to the LMT and continues to be an inspiration.

To Norbert Schiller whose stunning photographs helped me tell the story, especially when words were not enough; to the team: Christian Akhrass, Wim Balvert, Chamoun Mouannes and Lise-Lotte Sulukdjian whose companionship made this journey unforgettable; to our driver Sultan for always going the extra mile. Lastly Norbert and I would like to thank all our hosts, who welcomed us so warmly in their homes.

# Foreword

**When Hana Hibri** wrote asking that I lend my name to *A Million Steps,* I realized that, whether I liked it or not, I had become a rallying point for Lebanese who sought to embrace, enjoy and protect the outdoor opportunities and natural beauty of their country.

Although I didn't know Hana at all – and usually turn down such requests from strangers – I felt that on this occasion, it was my duty to go out of my way and lend my name to her project. The fact that I knew the LMT since its birth, and had biked across the length of the country along its beautiful trails, may have played a part in my decision. By and large, it was Hana's good vibes and the message she was trying to convey that were most influential.

It wasn't until several weeks later that I actually met Hana. She came up to me and introduced herself during a book signing event. Tall and lean, knowledgeable yet reserved, Hana appeared almost identical to how I imagined she would be. I exchanged stories and ideas with her and Mr. Hibri and I was subsequently happy to learn that the whole family was fond of nature and the mountains.

Not only did Hana find the time and will to walk across Lebanon from north to south, but she also chose to chronicle her journey. This yielded a document that is not just valuable in itself, but which can also spread the gospel of natural beauty, conservation, generosity of spirit, companionship, and personal achievement to people of all ages and nationalities.

I recommend this journey of *A Million Steps* to everyone, especially to those who are in search for renewed hope or answers. "When the feet move, the heart moves," said a wise man, who has since become more than a friend, and he did so while we trekked one of the trails of the LMT. It is for this reason that this short and pleasant story should be told through the eyes of this remarkable woman.

*Maxime Chaya*
*Beirut, February 19, 2010*

# A trail of hope

**My father** was born in Baskinta, the last village on the road leading from the coast just north of Beirut to the majestic Mount Sannine. He grew up there with his family in a time totally different from our own: before cars, before ski resorts, before air travel.

As a child and young man, he roamed Baskinta's valleys and mountains. Later as a husband and a father of six, he would take us on outdoor trips to hike, picnic and enjoy the same scenic and peaceful countryside that he had known as a child. My dad loved his hometown and the mountains of Lebanon, and he passed down this deep-rooted love to his children. Today, as he rests in peace next to the old church in the village he so cherished, my dad must rejoice at hearing the footsteps of hikers on the Lebanon Mountain Trail.

The Lebanon Mountain Trail is a fitting tribute to the millions of Lebanese who, like my father, have loved Lebanon and given her their best. Generation after generation, they have etched the natural landscape of the mountains with agricultural terraces, walking trails, and the places where they lived and worked, and played and mused. Generations of men and women, children and adults, followed those beaten footpaths to get to distant schools, meet loved ones, trade with their neighbors, and escape from invading armies on the coast. In their footsteps, people of all ages are now walking on the same trails for leisure, exploration, exercise, and rejuvenation.

The Lebanon Mountain Trail connects those old routes in one continuous 440-km (275-mile) hiking way stretching from North to South. It goes through or by: 75 towns and villages inhabited by nearly half-a-million people; three nature reserves (Horsch Ehden, Tannourine Cedar Reserve, and Al-Shouf Cedar Reserve); the World Heritage Site of Wadi Qadisha; numerous Ottoman castles; several ancient Roman ruins, bridges and rock inscriptions; the Khalil Gibran museum in Bsharreh; countless monasteries and churches; old water mills and silk factories; and other cultural landmarks. The LMT also has many side trails, such as the Baskinta Literary Trail, which celebrates the literary achievements of many writers and poets from this region, such as Mikhail Naimy, Amine Maalouf, and Abdallah Ghanem.

Increasing numbers of hikers and trekkers are discovering the Lebanon Mountain Trail, learning about the country and its rich history, culture, and landscapes. Over time, these visitors will help transform the economy of the Lebanese mountains, generating income and creating jobs locally, helping anchor the proud people of Lebanon in the land of their ancestors, and encouraging them to conserve their unique natural and cultural heritage. But one needs not be a hiker in order to take part in the wonderful LMT journey. In Lebanon, a non-profit, non-political Lebanese organization, the LMT Association, is working diligently with governmental and private organizations to protect, maintain and promote the trail as a world-class tourism destination.

In the United States, the American Friends of the Lebanon Mountain Trail has been established "to promote educational programs, environmental protection, natural and cultural heritage conservation and rural economic development related to and around the Lebanon Mountain Trail." Similar organizations are likely to sprout in the four corners of the world that have hosted the Lebanese Diaspora. Membership in, and support for, these organizations offer a unique opportunity for everyone to share the gift of the Lebanon Mountain Trail and to help unleash the unlimited opportunities made possible by it.

The Lebanon Mountain Trail invites us to honor and conserve the rich cultural and natural heritage of Lebanon's mountains, and to do our part, now and today, to ensure that those mountains' wonderful but limited natural resources are used in a manner consistent with our traditions, values and long-term interests. Together we can seize these opportunities, but we must act quickly before it is too late; before frenzied and unplanned development – as has happened on Lebanon's coast – irreversibly ravages the magic, beauty, serenity and harmony of the Lebanese mountains.

During his last days, at age 90, my father would struggle to reach the window of our Beirut apartment, standing there just long enough so he could take one more peek at the snow-capped Mount Sannine in the distance. You can take the boy out of the village, but you cannot take the village out of the boy. Like my dad, generations of Lebanese men and women, whether they come from mountain, coast, or plain, have passed along this unabated yearning of the hometown to their children and grandchildren. By hiking on the Lebanon Mountain Trail, and otherwise supporting the LMT Association and its partner organizations around the world, we honor the legacy of our forefathers and assert our stewardship of the Lebanese mountains, our right to enjoy them, and our duty to bequeath them to our children and to future generations to enjoy.

*Joseph Ghaleb Karam*
*CEO, ECODIT Group*
*President, American Friends of the LMT*

# Contents

# Introduction

It all started when I married Bassem and he took me on my first mountain adventure into the Rocky Mountains in Wyoming. After the first week of being miserable, I began to understand the lure of the mountains. I now realize I have always had ability to adapt (a valuable asset if you grow up as a diplomat's daughter and have to move from country to country).

But I have also always felt that if you can't leave your comfort zone, you miss out on new, exciting and rewarding experiences. Our most recent family adventure was an ascent of Mt. Kilimanjaro on December 31, 2007. When sharing the experience with friends and family, I noticed that the most common comment was, "Why would you put yourself through such extreme hardship? I could never do that." The truth of the matter is that the degree of exhilaration and euphoria of reaching the summit (or in general any goal) is proportionate to the difficulty of the challenge and hardship.

But it's not just about the destination. The journey and what you learn and take from it is equally important. I have also found that many people don't appreciate just how far determination can take you. It is usually far beyond what you perceive your limits to be.

Being an Arab and a mother of three, I recognize that my 'unconventional' pursuits do arouse people's interest and attention. In doing so, I hope that they may also inspire others to dare to leave their comfort zones and seek new challenges, even if it's just signing up for that exercise class they have been putting off.

So on to the book and this particular challenge. Why did I do it? Simply because it brought together so many things that are important to me: Lebanon's precious and unique mix of natural beauty and cultural heritage, an eco-system threatened by rampant quarries and improper garbage disposal (to name a few) and the desperate need for more extensive and forceful conservation efforts.

Coincidence? Chance? Luck? In the grand scheme of life I believe that all three are over-rated, while significant milestones and turning points are often dismissed as mere incidents. To say that everything in my life led me to undertake this exciting challenge would be an exaggeration, but I have no doubt that marrying a mountaineer who opened this world to me, my willingness to embrace new, challenging, not to mention, uncomfortable experiences, my love and dedication for this country and all the serendipitous encounters along the way have all pointed to this. All these thoughts rushed through me as I put my first foot forward. In so doing, I clocked up the first half meter.

There were only a million more steps to go.

*Hana El-Hibri,*
*Beirut, February, 2010*

*"Little by little, one travels far"*

J.R.R. TOLKIEN, *The Lord of the Rings*

# The adventure begins

Excitement and anxiety have kept me awake for most of the night, but the adrenaline compensates for the lack of sleep. The ministry of tourism is buzzing, but thankfully the press conference is brief. Due to a last minute change, Lise-Lotte[1] will be joining us! I am happy. Even though I am used to being the only woman on hikes, it will be great to have female companionship, especially someone with whom I get along so well. Lise-Lotte is like a ray of sunshine, a nickname that Norbert[2] and I give her for the trip.

We are eager to get going, and by 2 p.m. we pile into the bus parked off Hamra Street. As Sultan[3] helps us load the bags, I already regret all the "little extras" I have packed.

Driving north up the coastal highway, I look at the hundreds of billboards that use sex to sell everything from jeans to alcohol. They insult my intelligence and are a dangerous distraction for drivers.  But thanks to the lively conversation, I can ignore them and not get as infuriated as I usually do. North of Tripoli, Liselotte asks Sultan to stop so she can buy bananas (she always buys local or *baladi*, meaning of the country) from a roadside stall. Others follow her, while Norbert mutters about being in "Bananaland."

We head inland after Nahr El Bared[4] and I remember the battles in the summer of 2007 and the tragic loss of life. Christian[5] (aka Padre) points out the Syrian border and tells us that on a clear day you can see Le Krak Des Chevaliers, the famous Crusader fortress in the Syrian governorate of Homs. We reach the northernmost section of the Akkar region. Up ahead, rise the Qammoua Mountains, still snowcapped after the recent storm.

It is dusk when we arrive at Qbaiyat, which is actually six villages. It is enveloped in a soft haze. We stop at a *dekkaneh* for some last minute supplies. Chamoun[6] asks the shopkeeper to give him goods for free. At first I am taken aback and a bit embarrassed. But he later explains to me how his principle of hiking in the Lebanese mountains without any money is to prove the generosity and hospitality of the mountain people – a social experiment, as it were. He keeps detailed records of everyone who gives him something and will return after the trip and give them presents. Outside the store we bump into Ali Khalil, smartly dressed in his traditional baggy trousers or *sherwal*. He is our first encounter with the people who live on the trail, and, with typical village hospitality, he invites us to stay at his home in Akkar el Atiqa. He has the honor of being the first villager to sign our petition. One of the objectives of

Previous pages:
> THE CARMELITE MONASTERY OF MAR DOUMIT
> ALI KHALIL, AKKAR EL ATIQA
Below:
> MAR DOUMIT WITH QAMMOUA MOUNTAINS IN
THE DISTANCE

the thru-walk is to gather signatures for a petition to designate, through legislation, the LMT as a preserved area. A corridor running the length of Lebanon, protected from quarries, garbage dumping, unnecessary roads, unsightly construction and other eyesores and hazards. Nestled on a hill in the mist, overlooking the town is the Carmelite monastery of Mar Doumit, our home for the night.

The monastery is surrounded by towering cypress trees and in the courtyard is the Museum of Butterflies and Birds. We are told it was founded in 1973 by a private collector. The collection of local and foreign specimens is impressive.

The monks are at vespers but the caretaker takes us to our rooms. We have dinner at Karam's, a local restaurant. Ziad Faris, our guide for tomorrow, joins us but does not eat because he is observing lent, a reminder that religious and cultural traditions run strong in the mountains. Stars illuminate the brisk walk back to the monastery and it feels good to be back in the mountains.

Father Michel welcomes us warmly. He makes sure that we are comfortable and settled in for the night. Lise-Lotte and I are roommates. Our late-night conversations while lying in the dark seem more intimate than in the light of day. We talk about life, death, family and friendship. We talk about how privileged and excited we are to be part of this adventure and gradually lapse into the silence of our own thoughts.

-----------------------

[1] Lise-Lotte Sulukdjian (Danish) moved to Lebanon in 1975, after falling in love with her husband and the country. She is an experienced guide with Liban Trek and has hiked most of the LMT several times.
[2] Norbert Schiller (Austrian American) is a news photographer who has lived and covered the Middle East extensively for the past 29 years. His wife is Lebanese and he speaks Arabic. One of his great loves is hiking in the mountains, carrying a long staff fashioned out of a sturdy branch.
[3] Sultan, our bus driver, has many years experience driving in the Lebanese mountains.
[4] Palestinian refugee camp. Clashes in 2007 between the Lebanese Army and the Fatah El Islam militia resulted in loss of life on both sides as well as many civilians caught in the crossfire.
[5] Christian Akhrass is the organizer and leader of the Thru-walk. An experienced guide and environmental activist, he is also a member of the LMT Association and the Association Libanaise d'Etudes Spéléologiques (ALES).
[6] Chamoun Mouannes is a marathon runner who has also covered over 4,000km of Lebanon on foot.

"There is a phenomenon called Trail Magic,
known and spoken of with reverence... which
holds that often when things look darkest some
little piece of serendipity comes along to put
you back on a heavenly plane"

BILL BRYSON, *A Walk in the Woods*

The north

القبيات إلى تاشع

## Qbaiyat to Tashea
### Day 1

The beds were surprisingly comfortable last night. A luxury we will appreciate profoundly by the end of this trip. I wake up at 5 a.m. with that early-morning happiness. Father Raymond, the head monk, greets us for breakfast in the refectory, his serene face beaming. Elsewhere, everything is a bit fussy and erratic, as first days on long hikes usually are. Film crews from LBC and Al-Arabiya are also here to cover part of today's hike. As it turns out, Lutfallah[7] from LBC is Father Michel's cousin. Interesting, since Lutfallah is from Marjeyoun (our southern destination) and here we are in Qbaiyat. That's the way it is in Lebanon.

We set off. Wow, I am actually doing this! Walking the length of Lebanon. All 440 km[8] of it. I have no doubt I can do this. There can be no room for doubt when one undertakes a challenge like this. Doubt sets you up for discouragement and failure. There is a fear though. The fear that something might go wrong: an accident or illness. But these are beyond my control.

After a few kilometers, we reach the Byzantine monastery of Mar Chalita (Artemis) cradled in a flat stretch of land at the bottom of a valley. Rather uninteresting from afar, it is definitely

Previous pages:
> THE CHURCH OF SARKIS AND BAKHOS, AKKAR
Opposite:
> THE WATERFALL AT NABAA EL SHOUH
Below:
> HAMMOUD HAMMOUD, ZAWARIB
> HARF AKKAR, SHIR EL NIMRI
Next pages:
> OLD OAK GROVE, TASHEA

worth the detour. To enter into the temple, one must pass through a doorway with a very low portal. The inscription above reads 'Bow before your Lord, God,' which I find very symbolic.

The outer walls are ruins of a Roman temple while the tiny chapel is Byzantine. Inside, there are timeworn frescoes and icons. In the small garden surrounding the chapel there are stone presses and grinders. The monastery was self-sufficient. I wonder how old the huge olive trees are. Springs and streams are gushing with snowmelt. The fields are filled with cyclamen, anemones, wild orchids, daisies and many others whose names I don't know. Spring is in full swing.

We reach a clearing to find a pack mule grazing on freshly sprouted green grass. Padre and Norbert try to befriend it, but the animal is suspicious, kicking and charging at any opportunity. Its owner, Hammoud Hammoud, calls to us in that bellowing voice, so common to mountain folk who don't use telephones. I enjoy hearing him talk to Norbert: heavy Akkar accent versus Norbert's unique brand of Egyptian. Oh, I wish I had my recorder.

Even at 700m, it is hot. We peel off the extra layers and the trail through the densely wooded pine forest offers us a welcome

respite from the mid-morning sun. Ziad recommends we stop at the temple of Sarkis and Bakhos, where we lie under the canopy of huge oaks, refreshed by a soft cool breeze. The tell-tale vaults indicate that the Roman temple was converted to a church during Crusader times. Indeed, looking at our fair-skinned and red haired guide, the Crusaders weren't busy just building churches!

The trail follows the ridgeline of Harf Akkar. We take a mid-morning break on a massive slab of rock with breathtaking views of Akkar el Atiqa and its citadel. The snows of Qammoua seem very close now. I find Padre lovingly stroking a juniper tree. He tells me that the juniper (he calls it *habibti*) is his favorite tree and their berries, apart from used in the making of gin, have many medicinal qualities. He says this one is special because it is the first one he has seen on the hike.

The icy spring at Ain Shaito allows us to refill our water bottles. There we meet Hassan Al Masri, a shepherd with his flock and Toyyor, his dog. He uses an umbrella for a stick and is happy to pose for Norbert. He is amazed when we tell him of our 440km trip and invites us to spend the night at his house in Akkar el Atiqa. Toyyor is not as friendly as his master and ignores us.

By the time we get to the spring at Ain el Shouh, we are ravenous. The monks at Mar Doumit had packed sandwiches and Ziad shares his mother's homemade *zaatar* and *debs bi*

*tahineh.* Lying in the shade of more huge firs, we rest after an elevation gain of almost 1,000m. We have to shout over the roar of the gushing spring, but no one is talking really.

The hike to Tashea, our destination, is long (20 km) but not difficult. The dramatic cliffs of Qammoua are dotted with the deep green of firs. Padre decides to try a different route. He can do this, I suppose because he is Padre. He is the boss! But I am glad that he took us this way because we discover a cluster of massive oaks on a hilltop. We each find a spot to rest that is cradled by their magnificent trunks. Padre points out the small town of Tashea in the distance. Its most distinct features being it's church at one end and the mosque at the other - a microcosm of Lebanese coexistence. The encroaching road has eaten up this section of the trail and the last 3km are on asphalt.

Hiking down Tashea's only road, I am disturbed that there is hardly anyone around. There are no children playing or fields being tended to. There is no laundry being hung or invitation to coffee from an open doorway. The village is almost deserted, except for the small crowd of people gathered round a gas cylinder delivery truck near the mosque. Abu Marwan and his family are awaiting us at their doorstep as we hear the Adan[9] Asr.

What a very dusty and sweaty lot we are. However, they immediately make us feel at home in their modest but comfortable house. Showers but no booze. The area is very conservative and therefore "dry." Even though Norbert understands the customs of the area, he could have really used a cold beer. We sit on a vine-covered terrace sipping cold drinks: this is the life.

As squirrels cavort in the trees, a continuous stream of villagers pops in and out. The front door remains open as is customary in many village homes. Imm Marwan and her two daughters have prepared what I can only call a hearty dinner, such is our ravenous hunger from the day's exertions. It is just what we needed to prepare us for tomorrow's difficult hike. She proudly tells us that all the food is grown, raised or prepared by them.

It is quite remote here. The cell phone reception in Tashea is poor. The nearest grocer is a 10-minute drive away. There are no schools, doctors or pharmacies. Abu Marwan has eight children. Only his two young single daughters still live here. Because there are no schools in Tashea, all the young families have to move elsewhere. As a result, only 20% of the town still lives in the village. This is an unfortunate dilemma that many of the mountain villages face these days.

Writing my journal in the bedroom, I overhear Abu Marwan on the phone in the next room. I wasn't eavesdropping. He just talks really loudly.

Abu Marwan: *Allo*! How are you? Where are you? <pause> You need to come spend the evening with us <pause> No, you have to come. I have a houseful of *Ajeneb*[10] and I don't speak *Ajnabi*. You speak very well. I won't take no for an answer. *Yallah*, I'm waiting for you. Bye.

His "Ajnabi speaking" friend shows up shortly after and has a lengthy and animated conversation with Norbert (Nimsawi[11]) and Wim[12] (Hollandi[13]), much to the pleasure of Abu Marwan. In the meantime, the girls are taken by Chamoun's charm and colorful stories. Norbert and Wim decide to sleep on the terrace in their sleeping bags taking furtive swings from a concealed flask. I tell Norbert to beware that the squirrels don't get his nuts.

------------------------

[7] Lutfallah and his twin Karamallah are a freelance video/photography team, working mainly with LBC. Their company is called Twins Video, of course.
[8] The length of Lebanon (as the crow flies) is 220km but the LMT is 440km long.
[9] The five daily prayer times in Islam are announced by a call to prayer (Adan) from the mosque. Asr is mid-afternoon.
[10] *Ajnabi* (*ajeneb* pl.): Foreigner.
[11] Norbert's nickname, meaning Austrian in Arabic.
[12] Dutchman, Wim Balvert, an avid hiker, came all the way from Holland for the thru-walk. He is one of the core team of six.
[13] Wim's nickname, meaning Dutchman in Arabic.

*"My son has lost his mind"*

تاشع إلى القمامين

# Tashea to Qemmamine

## Day 2

Imm Marwan has prepared us a breakfast of *shanklish* and fried eggs. "To give you strength for your long hike today," she says. In the living room, Abu Marwan is showing off his hunting rifles to an early morning (7 a.m.) visitor. He is particularly proud of the custom-made pieces. They are gifts from his eldest son, who is in the army. He insists that I sit and have coffee with him. There is no sign of the daughters, who are still asleep. We tease Chamoun that it's his fault for keeping them up. He just smiles.

Our guide today is Mohamed from the neighboring town of Fnaydeq. He leads us to the overhanging cliffs of Qammoua and more sweeping vistas of the Akkar countryside below.

Previous pages:
> WATERFALL NEAR AIN EL KHOKH
> MOHAMED AYOUB EL AMERCANI, WADI HAKL
EL KHERBEH
Below:
> SYRIAN SPEEDWELL, VERONICA SYRIACA
> AT THE TOMB OF NABI KHALED

After a short climb, we reach a verdant plateau among softly rolling hills. We hike through a large meadow of purple and yellow wildflowers skirted by snowfields that literally mark the edge of spring. I find myself thinking with bewilderment, as I no doubt will countless times to come: Wow! This is in Lebanon?! The tomb of Nabi Khalid, a holy man of imposing physical stature, is situated on a flat saddle of land under the shade of two monumental iron oaks.

We opt for a small detour off the trail to visit the amazing 'enchanted' Azre forest. This rare forest of iron oaks is the only one of its kind in Lebanon. Covering several hectares of woodland, its winter-dead trees rise 20m to 30m. Standing in their midst one half-expects to see some fairytale creature pop out. It would make a great setting for a C.S. Lewis or Tolkien story.

At lunch, we nibble on our trail mix of nuts and dried fruit, resting against the twisted trunks of junipers. It never ceases to amaze me how frequently, and within such a short space of time, the scenery changes: the color of the soil, the trees and flowers, the rock, moving from soft hills to dramatic gorges.

Padre and Lise-Lotte had warned us in our daily briefing the night before of a grueling downhill slog. We are about to find out they weren't kidding. The descent commences gradually. To our right is a picturesque valley with abandoned amphitheatre-like terraces. Then the incline becomes steeper, and the trail rockier and more uneven as we descend deeper into the gorge. The striking cliffs surrounding us provide visual distraction from our sore knees. Long downhills are a killer and we perversely find ourselves wishing for a bit of uphill. It takes us three bone-jarring hours to descend the 1,000m to the bottom of the valley of Wadi Mgharet El-Tibn.

Rockslides and rapid erosion have covered most of the trails since our guide was here last. The problem is not only finding the trail but figuring out at which point we can cross the raging river, swollen from the melting snow. Mohamed and Lise-Lotte consult for a while and decide on a route that involves quite a bit of bushwhacking. After a few minutes and even more scratches, we encounter a man on a donkey coming up a path with two children in tow. Mohamed Ayoub El Amercani (the American) is flustered and agitated. "You will forgive me if I don't welcome you properly but there has been a catastrophe at home," he tells us. It is wonderful and touching that he not only feels it his obligation to extend his hospitality and all the appropriate courtesies to visitors in his valley, but that he apologizes in advance if he is unable to do so. When I ask what the catastrophe is, he answers, "My son has lost his mind."

He hastily advises us as to which crossing to take and instructs us to follow him till the fork in the path so we don't get lost again. He whips the donkey up the narrow footpath, with the two speechless children scrambling behind him in the dust, to what I presume is his house (there are only two homes visible in the entire valley and surrounding mountainside). We are left standing there, feeling pretty much the way Alice must have felt after her first encounter with the Mad Hatter. We head on down the path to the next item on our obstacle course. The river crossing…

The waters are quite high, and we must take off our boots to wade across. The freezing water increases my resolve not be toppled, boots, pack and all, into the shallow but raging torrent. Chamoun extends a walking stick that I grasp tightly. Numb feet on slippery pebbles are not the best combination for crossing a torrent. Amazingly, I make it to the other side with only a few minor cuts. I am more drenched than anything else. Thank God for quick-drying fabric.

The terraced valley narrows, giving way to massive limestone cliffs. Flanking the sides of one of the most impressive gorges I have ever seen, we hike in speechless wonder, dwarfed and humbled by the scale of the canyon.

> LOOKING OUT FROM THE FNAYDEQ PINE FOREST:
QORNET EL ASHRA (LEFT) AND HARF EL QANDIL (RIGHT)

On reaching the Nabaa el Tine spring, it becomes apparent that our second river crossing is going to be even trickier. At this point, the current is so strong that wading is not an option, and it is now a matter of finding the best spot to jump across. Mohamed leaps nimbly from one huge boulder to the next and helps the rest of us in the crossing. Having the shortest legs in the group, I am apprehensive. It's not so much being scared of getting hurt as the prospect of not being able to continue. After much coaxing and encouragement from Norbert and my long-legged Lise-Lotte, I take a leap of faith. It is not one of my most graceful moments. I come close to having my face flattened against a boulder, but I get away with only a badly bruised knee and more minor scrapes.

Following the course of the river, the seemingly endless downhill path along Wadi Hakl el Kherbeh finally leads us to the village of Qemmamine. For us by-now-hardened river-crossers, negotiating the precarious log bridge is easy.

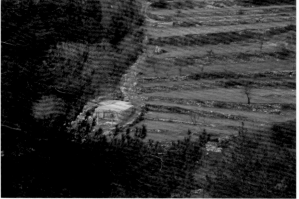

Qemmamine is the remotest village reachable by paved road in the area. It is dusk and we are greeted by a group of children who insist on carrying our packs. We also got what we wished for: a nice steep 300m uphill to the home of Abou Khalid Issa, who welcomes us with a toothless smile.

Due to his freakishly fast pace, Chamoun has the advantage of getting first digs at the shower. He is Marathon Man after all, and is already hanging his laundry by the time we get in. I nudge Lise-Lotte, saying, "Look, he is hanging out his red underwear." She gets a mischievous glint in her eye, but I've no idea what she is up to.  Shortly later she tells me to check out the clothesline. Hanging next to the red underwear is a RED LACE BRA!

Abu Khalid's beautiful daughters, Fatima and Ruwaida, have cooked for us. Like most women in this area they wear headscarves and refuse to have their picture taken, much to Norbert's dismay. I am surprised that I have never tasted many of the delicious dishes laid out before us. I love eating on the

floor! Afterwards, one can just roll over and lapse comfortably into a food coma.

Qemmamine must be at the thin end of the electricity supply. The current is weak and we keep our flashlights and headlamps handy. I am delighted that, despite the long power cut, we still had hot water for showers, courtesy of solar water heaters. The group that will be joining us for the weekend arrives from Beirut at around 7:30 p.m. Bassem[14] is very excited about being here.

We walked 24km. It has been a long day and we all blissfully snuggle in our sleeping bags. All of us except for Marathon Man, that is, who is still chatting away to the captive audience of the two sisters long after everyone is asleep.

"Wait till you see the view from our room tomorrow morning!" I tell Bassem before we sleep.

------------------------
[14] Hana's husband.

*"Oh, that's just to keep the rats out"*

القمامين إلى كفربنين

# Qemmamine to Kfar Bnine

## Day 3

I wake up to a nagging pain in my stomach, which I put down to overeating. It's 3 a.m. and through the window I can see a spectacular night sky.

What remains of the night is fitful at best and I'm wide-awake when the first stirrings of morning begin. Bassem looks out the window overlooking the valley and is amazed at the dramatic gorge and surrounding peaks.

The name Qemmamine has evolved from Qemmam (peaks) Amine, or Amine's peaks. We have breakfast in the family's *ouda shatwiyyeh,* or winter room, with a wood burning cast iron stove, or *sobia*, in the center. There is tea brewing in the kettle on the stove. Imm Khalid pours and I sip it slowly, hoping it will help settle my stomach.

We meet up with rest of the group and our local guide, Ahmad El Kik, at the other guesthouse. The ascent to Maaboor el Eezre is immediately taxing. The steep 700m climb seems practically vertical. Bassem, who is usually up front with the faster paced hikers, can tell something's not right and stays with me. The harder I breathe, the sharper and

more frequent the pains become, and Bassem makes me take frequent stops to rest and drink.

Padre and Lise-Lotte are also concerned and arrange to meet with Sultan on a dirt road not far from the trail. There is no way I can finish the day's hike in my condition. We reach the summit huffing and puffing, but what really takes our breath away is the view: a panorama of numerous peaks, gorges, valleys and rivers.

And then the fog starts rolling in, bringing with it a familiar chill.

Sultan is at the meeting point by the time we get there. The drive to Kfar Bnine is on a long and very windy road that goes down a steep valley and then up the other side. It does not help my nausea and dizziness. I keep pushing the idea that I might not be able to continue this adventure to the back of my mind. I don't want to deal with that possibility now.

The seemingly endless, hour-long, drive ends in the quiet village of Kfar Bnine. Sultan pulls up into the driveway of an abandoned house[15]. Surely, he must be mistaken. The shutters are warped and overgrown weeds suggest that this place hasn't been inhabited recently. Sultan assures me that he has already checked the address twice. He calls the owner on his cell phone and we wait for half an hour for him to come in from his fields. He seems bothered by our early arrival and in a rush to get back to work.

"Nice set for a horror movie," I think, "but where is the film crew?" We enter through the creaking door. As we follow him around for the grand tour, our footsteps leave tracks in a thick layer of dirt and dust. Dust, I will later find out, will be the least of our worries. I inspect the bathroom and immediately regret it. When I ask Abu Walid why there is a big rock covering the drain in the sink he says, "Oh, that's just to keep the rats out." Great! I think I'll stick to using my hand sanitizer. He pulls out a dubious looking blanket from a cupboard. His daughter will come by at around 3 p.m. o'clock to give us the rest of the linens, he says, and then leaves. I can't wait.

The fog is swirling in from cracked windows. I choose the least drafty of the three bedrooms and the bed that looks the least likely to collapse. We lay the blanket on the dusty bed, my sleeping bag on top and I crawl in. Sultan makes me a cup of

tea from his supplies. His bus is so well equipped and stocked that we joke that the only things he still needs are a bathroom and microwave. He gives me his cell number in case I need anything.

I am alone, and with the sound of his last footsteps, I feel the utter silence of the place. No passing cars, children playing, chickens clucking, dogs barking. Nothing. Well, at least the scurrying noises under the rock inside haven't started… yet.

Lying here in pain and alone in this nightmare of a house, I struggle with the urge to feel sorry for myself. Fatigue finally overcomes my increasingly overactive imagination and I doze off into a restless sleep.

I wake to the sound of people talking and boots trudging up the stairs. My hiking buddies are here! They each come in to check on me and give me encouragement and reassurance. The bathroom is so dirty that nobody even bothers to ask if there is hot water for showers. We skip our daily routine of changing into clean clothes at the end of the day.

We all gather in the "living room" and the lively conversation cheers me up a bit. Norbert tells me that he was disappointed not being able to capture the spectacular view from the plateau overlooking the dramatic valley. It was completely backlit by the sunrise. They hiked through a beautiful green meadow to the second stage of their climb. Padre was so excited by all the junipers in the mist. He picked up a small piece and attached it to his pack so that its fragrance could accompany him all day. Norbert was happy with all the shepherds they encountered, sometimes

walking through an entire herd. They were on their yearly migration to higher pastures. The later it got, the thicker the fog became, and with it a light but steady drizzle.

But the truth is that rest hasn't helped my condition and my anxiety about tomorrow is mounting. I decide to call Dr. Nuhad, our family doctor. His diagnosis is "nervous stomach." When I think of it now, the month leading up to this trip has been a very anxious time for me. I guess you can be anxious even if you are excited and happy. Dr. Nuhad prescribes some medicine and says I should be all right by tomorrow evening. There's only one problem: the nearest pharmacy is half an hour away, it is dark and the fog is thick. Sultan has overheard the conversation and insists on getting me the medicine. If he were not such an excellent driver, I wouldn't let him make such a dangerous drive. Nemir, one of the newcomers, thoughtfully offers to keep him company.

They are back in an hour and just in time for dinner at the house of Khalid El Sayed, tomorrow's guide. I suspect that the rather lengthy candle lit dinner is due to our reluctance to go back to the "house." Sleeping arrangements are rather cozy, 12 people in three tiny rooms. Somehow, Padre ends up in the middle room with four women.

The dreaded trip to the bathroom in the middle of the night: navigating in the dark, using the flashlight sparingly so as not to blind sleeping bodies is tricky at best. I'm in. Why did I just lock the door? It's the same stupid reflex that causes you to turn on the light switch when you know there's no electricity. I'm so proud that I manage to finish without falling into the hole-in-the-ground toilet at such record speed. And then my heart sinks. The door won't open. I coax the key, patiently and quietly at first, and then the prospect of spending the night with the "drain residents" freaks me out and my attempts become more desperate. From the other side of the door I hear a whisper. It is Bassem. "Are you OK?" he asks. "Yes, but the f*****g door is stuck," I hiss. The situation is rapidly becoming Clouseau-esque with us both scrambling around in the dark.

Finally, the door opens with a creak as loud as the house is quiet. Mortified that someone may have heard my embarrassing episode, I'm hugely relieved that everyone seems fast asleep.

-----------------------

[15] The house in Kfar Bnine is not used as a guesthouse. Due to unforeseen complications, it was the only available option at the time of the thru-walk. All villages on the LMT offer decent accommodations for hikers.

"i am bored out of my mind"

كفربنين إلى بقاعصفرين

# Kfar Bnine to Bqaa Sefrine
## Day 4

In the morning, my anxieties are realized. "Who was that knocking down the bathroom door in the middle of the night?" someone asks. Another voice: "I don't know, but it was such a racket it woke us up."

I carry on packing in silence.

It is becoming apparent to me that I won't be well enough to hike today and I can't disguise my disappointment. The team gives me extra strong hugs of encouragement, and tells me to hurry up and get better. *Inshallah.* Watching them hiking up the mountain, I realize how badly I want to be with them. I promise myself that I will come back later and hike this portion of the trail, but it won't be the same.

One of the great things about Sultan is he knows when to be chatty and when to leave you alone with your thoughts. Thus, it is a quiet drive to the beautiful and historic town of Sir ed Danniye, even if, a few years ago it became known as a hotbed for Islamist fundamentalists. But today, it appears rather peaceful as far as hotbeds go.

Previous page:
> ONE OF HUNDREDS
Opposite:
> NABAA ES SUKKAR
> ALONG THE WATER CANAL LEADING TO BQAA SEFRINE
Below:
> HUSSEIN AND HARBA LEJA, FARMERS FROM SFIRE
Next pages:
> ROCK OVERLOOKING QARSAITA

Road signs here are either non-existent or misleading at best, so we are at the mercy of the directions of residents, who appear either a bit soft in the head or deliberately messing with us. After three failed attempts, we finally find the turn off to Bqaa Sefrine. The address we have is simple: Abu Majed's house, Bqaa Sefrine. The *dekkaneh* owner in the town square points to the road heading up the mountainside, "Up there. It's the three-storey gray building." Of the five buildings fitting that description, we get lucky at the second attempt.

We enjoy a *soubhiyyeh*, sitting in the sun and sipping Imm Majed's mint tea. Abu Majed's chickens join us. It is the most comical and ridiculous looking bunch of chickens I have ever seen. From feather-padded feet and random bald patches to unruly tufts of head feathers. God definitely has a sense of humor on this day.

Abu Majed Sayyah and his younger son are building a house next door. They are doing all the work themselves, he tells me

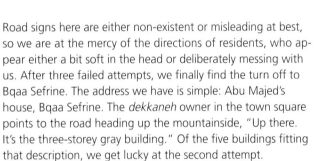

Previous pages:
> BASSEM CONTEMPLATING THE CLIFFS OF NABAA
ES SUKKAR
Below:
> GUSHING STREAM FROM NABAA ES SUKKAR
Opposite:
> AHMED EL SAYYED. THE VILLAGE BUTCHER OF
KFAR BNINE
> NOF KASSEM SOUAK, WHOSE FATHER WAS A REBEL
IN THE STRUGGLE FOR INDEPENDENCE IN 1943
> BREAK ON THE CLIFF

proudly. He just hires people to do the plumbing and electrical work. A family from the Gulf has been renting one of the apartments for the entire summer and needed more space. This is a significant source of income for Abu Majed. The tenant loves this area so much that he decided to reforest the entire mountainside with indigenous cypress at his expense. I am both touched that a foreigner would undertake a project like this and dismayed that there aren't more Lebanese who care this much. Abu Majed remembers a time when the whole mountain was densely forested. Forest fires claimed part, the rest cut down for firewood. In many of these impoverished areas, rising fuel costs and a minimal electricity supply leave the villagers with few other options during the cold winter months. Even though I am outraged at them for abusing our beautiful forests, I also feel the country has failed them by not providing alternatives.

This will probably be the only time that I beat Chamoun to the shower. Arefa, Majed's new wife invites me to her apartment below, since the one we will be staying in is still being cleaned. CLEAN – music to my ears.

Clean and dry I join the family. Arefa insists on doing my laundry herself. She and her two young sisters-in-law join me in the sitting room. Even though I am aching to be out hiking with the rest, I feel I am getting a privileged glimpse into the daily lives of this family. Arefa is pregnant. She is Imm Majed's niece. The daughters help their mom with chores when they're not in school. They ask inquisitive questions about me, the LMT and what on earth possessed me to undertake this folly. They watch Egyptian soap operas while I catch up on my journal writing. When they're done, Arefa looks out the window, lets out a long heavy sigh and says, "I am bored out of my mind." There isn't much to do for young women in these villages. The daily routine is usually: housework, watching T.V. and receiving visitors. Most of the husbands commute to work in the cities. They leave very early in the morning and come home quite late.

It's mid-afternoon and I'm restless. Sitting outside with the Sayyah's and their visitors I keep glancing at the path to see if there are any hikers coming. And then I see two red specks in the distance. Chamoun's signature flags! Of course he would be the first one to appear. It's only been a few hours but I am

so excited to see them and hear about today's adventure. By the time the group gets in I am feeling much better. Most of the day's hike was along a long system of irrigation canals and it was mostly uphill. They met many farmers and their families tending orchards. One spot was particularly beautiful: a rock that overlooked an entire valley. Ah well, at least I can look forward to Norbert's photos. Norbert and Chamoun tell me, with great annoyance, about a group of hunters stuck in the snow. They were loud, obnoxious and had no business being there to begin with. One of them had the gall to ask Norbert if they could use his staff to try and wedge out his Range Rover. He would have had better luck asking him for a hundred bucks.

The weekenders leave us today, but a young Frenchman joins us. Severin learnt about the thru-walk by chance on the internet and spontaneously decided to join us for three days. I am very pleasantly surprised at the interest the thru-walk has generated with overseas hikers. Apart from Wim (Hollandi), our core-team member, and Severin there will be five other foreigners flying in to join us at different stages of the trek. It proves that eco-tourism is an important part of the tourism sector in Lebanon that should not be neglected.

Padre gives us the nightly briefing on tomorrow's hike, which will end in Horsh Ehden, one of eight nature reserves in the country. "They make good arak in Ehden," Norbert comments, happy that the 'dry spell' is almost over. He knows a thing or two about arak, having worked on a book called *Arak and Mezze*.

Norbert and Wim come in from an evening stroll and visit with Lise-Lotte and me in our room. Norbert is cracking us up with jokes, and I suspect at least part of his good humor is coming from the little flask in his jacket. We kick them out when we get sleepy, but the laughter has done me good. I am glad to have my roommate Lise-Lotte all to myself tonight. We talk about the power of positive thinking and attitude, very relevant after my discouraging past two days. Before dozing off, I say a little prayer for tomorrow.

"For lo, the winter is past, the rain is over and gone;
The flowers appear on the earth; the time of the
singing birds is come, and the voice of the turtle is
heard in our land"

THE SONG OF SOLOMON

بقاعصفرين إلى إهدن

# Bqaa Sefrine to Ehden
## Day 5

Abu Majed's roosters have no concept of time. I decide that it is only in cartoons that they crow when the sun comes up. Lying in bed at 3 a.m., I can also hear a strong gusting wind picking up outside and hope that my laundry won't be blown away. Lise-Lotte has this amazing ability to get dressed, pack, wash and basically be ready to go without making a sound. I make more noise just turning over in bed. She reassures us that since the wind is blowing from the mountains, we won't be getting rain today. The tiny clothespins have withstood the winds, but in my rush to get out of the cold I lose a pair of undies. Looking down in dismay as they flutter hastily down to the Sayyah's terrace below, I am relieved that they are not early risers.

A quick breakfast and we are on our way through the blossoming pear orchards below. A dirt road leads us around a mountainside wooded with cypress trees. We stop to chat with an old man pruning trees in his orchard. Hassan Hammoud is from the town of Assoun. He explains that the name of the town means 'the rebellious.' He says it with pride and a twinkle in the eye.

We are now heading to the higher elevations of the *jurd* (high-lands). The vegetation is getting more arid. The rocky hillsides are strewn with shrubs, bushes and the occasional, solitary oak. The trail seems to have the capacity to continuously change and sur-prise for there, nestled in the cusp of the mountain pass, are bright green wheat fields. Stunningly contrasted against the rugged landscape, they are reminders that spring is here. Trekking through green terraces we reach the Roman ruins of Douraya. We explore the scattered ruins overgrown with *andoul* (spartium, aka Spanish broom) and the burial site of a local no-table, Sheikh Abdullah. Under the breezy shade of two more monumental oaks we have a short, but energizing break.

A dusty footpath leads down into the valley and to a sunlit glade, where a babbling brook – the spring of Ain Douraya – empties into a series of placid pools of crystal clear water. We

fill our water bottles amid a chorus of crickets and frogs. It's really hard to leave this tranquil spot but the long road ahead beckons and we are immediately greeted by a steep climb. As soon as we crest the ridge of the mountain the wind picks up significantly. Lunch is a windy affair in the scanty shelter of a lone juniper (at least Padre is happy), but it gives us time to contemplate how untamed and beautiful our surroundings are. The landscape is unlike anything I have ever seen in Lebanon: very rocky and rugged with only a spattering of the occasional windswept oak or snow-white khokh el dib[16] tree. For as far as the eye can see, there are no signs of encroaching urbanization. We haven't encountered a soul on the trail for the past five hours. I truly feel the remoteness of the area.

From a distance, we can make out the dark entrance of *Mgharet el Hawa,* or wind cave, peering out from the snow-field. All year, a continuous wind blows out from the kilometer deep cave. At 1,820m, the spring that is connected to the cave is one of the highest in the country. Parched from the dryness at this altitude, we try to refill our bottles between ice, slick rocks and gushing water.

The rest of the day's hike is deep snow. Marathon Man puts on his galoshes and opens a path in the snow. Struggling with soft snow and high winds is exhausting, but we plod on. As the wetness begins to set in my boots, I curse myself for leaving my gaiters in the bag. The wetness is turning cold and my feet become numb. Crossing the boundary of the Horsh Ehden Nature Reserve, we are struck by the serenity and majesty of its trees. In the snowfields are patches of delicate spring blossoms.

Previous pages:
> PASSING BY THE FAMOUS CEDAR ON THE WAY TO
NABAA EL HAWA
Opposite:
> ANDOUL, *SPARTIUM*
Below:
> TERRACED ORCHARDS ON THE WAY TO KARM
EL MOHR

We have also seen many tortoises today. Norbert comments
on their precarious mating habits, especially with so many haz-
ardous cliffs around. This reserve is very rich in bio-diversity.
Over 1,030 plant species have so far been recorded in the reserve, accounting for nearly 40% of the plant species in
Lebanon, 115 of which are indigenous. More than 26 mammals have also been sighted in the reserve (not including bats),
representing a third of the mammals in Lebanon.

The last portion of the trail leading to the reserve's visitor center
is a hilltop of shoulder high grass. The sweet scent of the radiant
yellow andoul plant has accompanied us for most of the day. As
we see the log cabins through the trees, our pace quickens with
the prospect of hot showers and clean, dry clothes.

There is a 'welcome party' made up of the reserve manager, the
Twins Video crew, Sultan and assorted staff. This is off-season

Opposite:
> THE NORTHERN BORDER OF HORSH EHDEN NATURE RESERVE
> LISE-LOTTE HEADING UP TO HORSH EHDEN
> LONELY CEDAR TREE
Next pages:
> ROMAN RUINS AT SHEIKH ABDULLAH

and we are the only guests staying, not that we really mind. We already have that comfortable familiarity that develops on long hiking trips. There is a special bond that forms when you share a trekking experience. After much huffing and puffing, Lise-Lotte and I lug our bags up the stairs to our 'log' cabin. We discover that they have overlooked turning on the water heater and we settle for just piling on more layers since it's getting really cold fast.

We meet for dinner in the dining room and huddle around the cast iron wood-burning stove. The room is... ahem... eclectic in its décor: red gingham curtains, stuffed deer heads, Indian dream catchers and Christmas decorations. The Lent *mezza* is delicious and the guys festively break their dry spell with some local arak.

The Lebanese are so accustomed to power cuts that there is hardly a pause in the conversation when the generator breaks down. After attempts by the staff to fix it fail, Lutfallah and Karamallah jump into action. A considerable amount of elbow grease (literally) later, the generator splutters back to life.

Back in our cabin, we meet the locals: spiders, centipedes and daddy long legs. They are very welcome to shack up with us. I am too tired to care.

------------------------

[16] Bear plum, *Prunus ursina*.

"The whole canyon holds its spell from sea to mountains like a meditation on the majesty of God, and finds its end in the Wadi Qadisha, the 'Holy Valley,' where between rock and air, Byzantine monks built monasteries, and hermits scooped their grottos from the cliffs"

COLIN THUBRON, *The Hills of Adonis*

إهدن إلى وادي قاديشا
# Ehden to Wadi Qadisha
## Day 6

Temperatures drop to single digits overnight and Lise-Lotte and I decide that our sleeping bags are as good a place as any to get dressed. The commotion we heard during the night was made by the twins, Lutfallah and Karamallah, battling a burst water pipe that soaked their cabin. You have to be really good-natured to be able to laugh something like that off in the morning.

Today's relatively short 10km hike allows us the luxury of a more leisurely pace to our morning preparations. The bus drops us off at the monastery of Mar Yaacoub or St Jacob, on the outskirts of the town of Ehden. The shrine overlooks a gently terraced green valley. The lofty snow-capped summits of distant mountains to the east peek out through the morning mist. It is a short walk to church of Mar Moura, where we start our descent into the village of Aintourine perched in a valley known as Wadi Qozhaya.

Reaching a clearing of old stone houses, we meet Ishak, aka Abu Joseph, on his way to his orchards, effortlessly balancing a hoe on his shoulder. His deep blue eyes sparkling from his delightfully weathered face, he bids us Godspeed. An old watermill

overgrown with ivy and blossom presages a waterfall, spray that is so strong we are forced to put on our raingear and tuck away our cameras. Progress down its steep slick sides is slow and deliberate. I am astounded at how many new spring flowers we have seen today. As we progress further down into the valley the trees thin out. The steep mountain face to our right is speckled with caves, many of which were homes to hermits. The inaccessibility of the Qozhaya and Qadisha valleys, with their numerous caves and grottos were an ideal haven for the ascetic hermits and monks, as well as patriarchs fleeing religious persecution.

Previous pages:
> RUINS OF MAR ABOUN, WADI QADISHA
Opposite:
> CHARBEL NOHRA AT MAR ANTONIOS QOZHAYA
> NORBERT'S FAN CLUB
> WATER MILL OF AINTOURINE
> VALERIANA

## MAR ANTONIOS QOZHAYA

Sitting precariously on the side of the mountain, the monastery of Mar Antonios Qozhaya houses the oldest Syriac printing press in the world, dating back to 1600. Father Michel welcomes us at the entrance and gives us a tour of the museum and church located on the upper courtyard. Half of the church is actually a large grotto in the rock. He also shows us a big cave where insane people and 'undesirables' were incarcerated. The shackles, cuffs and chains, still scattered about, conjure up rather disturbing images.

Wadi Qannoubine is even more dramatic than Qozhaya: the valley is lined with precipitous cliffs of multi-colored rock interspersed with countless gushing waterfalls that end in a verdant and lush valley floor. The old stone homes in the valley are all built in the same style: a simple, rectangular floor plan with flat thatched roofs for stone rolling. Some are abandoned and in ruin, some vacant till summer, while only a few are lived in year round. The entire, 13km valley, a World Heritage Site, is accessible only by foot.

The trails are mainly donkey and goat paths, and as we round a bend, we encounter a very large herd of goats relaxing among the rocks. Norbert, who was a goat-herder in Greece in a previous life, is quick with his camera. I'm not quite sure if the goats feel the love or just like having their picture taken, but the entire herd simultaneously turns and looks at him. We are all in stitches. Further up the valley, we encounter a group of French tourists having a picnic lunch at one of the many ruins along the trail. Marathon Man goes over and talks to them, but the rest of us trudge along up the trail. We're tired and hungry.

We eat lunch on a soft cushion of pine needles overlooking the peaceful valley. Even Padre is reluctant to get up from his catnap. The rest of the trail, to Abu Joseph's restaurant/guesthouse, is a covered canal. Sunlight filtered through the overhead branches throws spotlights on the path. Abu Joseph's is unreachable by car, and all supplies are shuttled from the dirt road by pushcart. The shuttle service is usually handled by Jumaa[17], Abu Joseph's Man Friday, who is at once gardener, housekeeper, mechanic, concierge and waiter. He has an incredible knack for being around wherever and whenever he is needed.

Severin thanks us for the trip, which he calls 'a gift' and reluctantly bids us farewell. He promises to come back at the first opportunity. The mouth-watering aromas coming out of Imm Joseph's kitchen don't make his departure any easier. He hikes up to the meeting point where his taxi is waiting, accompanied by, of course, Jumaa.

-----------------------
[17] *Jumaa:* Arabic for Friday. It is also given as a name.

"And this our life, exempt from public haunt,
Finds tongues in trees, books in the running brooks,
sermons in stones, and good in everything"

WILLIAM SHAKESPEARE, *As You Like It*

قاديشا

# Qadisha - Rest day

Day 7

We wake up to a chorus of chirping birds and the heavenly scent of sweet pastries. Upstairs, Imm Joseph is baking up a storm for Easter Sunday and it occurs to me that the tradition of making *maamoul* on religious feasts is common to both Lebanon's Christians and Muslims. Vasso[18] joins us for breakfast, while Rocky, a rambunctious and friendly Jack Russell puppy, appears on the sunny upper terrace. He takes a particular liking to Norbert who says, "Yeesss Rocky. You like us *ajeneb*. We treat you well and love you. We treat you so well, we even pick up your poop."

## THE MONASTERY OF OUR LADY OF QANNOUBINE

Clouds are beginning to roll in and we decide to make an early start of our visit to the monasteries and hermitage in the area. We backtrack along the water canal and take the trail up to the Monastery of Our Lady of Qannoubine. Lise-Lotte goes ahead to get the key to the monastery from Abu Charbel. Nuns stay here in the summer. The rest of the year, Abu Charbel is the 'keeper of the key' and caretaker/guardian. The monastery was the seat of the Maronite patriarchy for over 400 years. Built partially into the rock, it has many simple, but beautiful frescoes inside the chapel.

## THE CHAPEL OF SAINT MARINA

Nearby is the chapel/grotto of Saint Marina, which houses her
tomb and those of over 20 patriarchs. The inscriptions are in a
very special Syriac script. During the Ottoman rule, this script was
developed so that it would easily be mistaken for Arabic. Lise-
Lotte recounts one of the versions of the legend of Saint Marina:

Marina's mother died when she was a young child. Her grief
stricken father decided to become a monk and entrusted Marina to the care of her aunt. When he returned to see her after
many years, she told him that she wanted to join him. She insisted so much that finally her father conceded. He took her dis-
guised as a boy back with him to the monastery, where she
spent many years known as brother Marin. While on a mission,
'Brother Marin' spent the night in the home of a family. Shortly
after, the daughter got pregnant and accused Brother Marin of
being the father. Marina accepted the responsibility and raised
the child in the monastery. It was not until her death that it was
discovered that she was a woman. She was canonized for her
sacrifice, and for bearing the shame and sins of another.

Previous pages:
> CLIFFS NEAR THE HAWQA HERMITAGE
Opposite:
> MONASTERY OF OUR LADY OF QANNOUBINE
Below:
> ANEMONES

## HAWQA HERMITAGE

I am really excited about meeting the Columbian hermit, Dario Escobar, who lives alone in the Hawqa hermitage. He has been living here since 2000 and speaks eight languages fluently. Lise-Lotte pushes me to the front of the group. "He's more likely to come out of his quarters if he sees a woman," she says. "He enjoys chatting with the ladies."

The steep and narrow trail is squeezed between the rock face on the right and sheer cliffs to the left. This is not a trail for the faint-hearted. The more scary parts have roping for protection. The hermitage is built under an impressive rock overhang. As we get closer, we respect the signs for silence. The hermitage is basically a series of grottos that have been closed off. We notice one of the rooms has a light on, but brother Escobar is nowhere to be found. I am disappointed to have missed him, but this fascinating place was well worth the visit. I can always come back.

Lise-Lotte tells us that Abu Charbel and his wife insisted we stop by for coffee on our way back. They are waiting for us outside their typical Qadisha Valley home and greet us with big, warm toothless smiles. They have lived here all their lives, but their five children have left. Some immigrated while the rest live in villages above the valley. It is fava bean planting season, but Abu Charbel is only working the fields near the house where the wild boars have not dug up his crop. Imm Charbel sits next to him on the edge of the bed and he tenderly puts his arm around her shoulders. She asks Lise-Lotte if she would like to make the coffee, "ala zaw'ik, or your way. Her eyesight is failing and this is a subtle way for her to ask Lise-Lotte for help.

Vasso and I pick wild thyme on the way back, from which Abu Joseph makes a simple but excellent salad. Not used to *mezze* lunches anymore, we pass out in our rooms. The afternoon showers come and we brace ourselves for tomorrow's long up-hill hike in the rain.

------------------------

[18] Lise-Lotte's husband is a pilot, hardcore hiker, mountain biker and speleologist.

"In the sweetness of friendship let there be laughter, and sharing of pleasures. For in the dew of little things the heart finds its morning and is refreshed"

KHALIL GIBRAN

قاديشا إلى الأرز
# Qadisha to the Cedars
## Day 8

I awake at 5 a.m. and listen for the patter of rain, but there is complete silence. Lise-Lotte persuades me to come outside for some stretching and warm-ups. The small patio is dimly lit by a halo of light from the single light post, and a faint ethereal mist lingers in the valley. We go through her routine, quiet as mice (even though the unlikely passerby would probably think we were nuts). Back in our room, we hear the first morning stirrings in the valley. We are up before the birds!

As we set off, we learn that snow has also fallen at our destination in the Cedars. Meanwhile, trees with bright green spring buds are glistening in the morning sun. Countless waterfalls on both sides of the valley have deeply grooved the rock face and created fantastic formations, caves and grottos. We pass by the monastery of Mar Lichaa. Initially inhabited by a hermit in the 14th century, it has been in continuous use by hermits and monks ever since.

With an elevation of 1,000m, the steep trail leads us up out of the valley to the village of Bcharre perched at 1,400m. As we near the crest, our guide, Tony, tells us that in the Qadisha Valley it was customary for the locals to put their boys through a light-hearted coming-of-age test to see if they were ready for marriage. The young men were given two buckets of milk to carry out of the valley. If they were able to do this without stopping or spilling any milk, they were eligible.

We encounter a herd of goats. Their owner Youssef, from Bcharre el Arz, tells us that he has to stay close to his flock because there has been a recent spate of goat thefts. He says he knows who the culprits are, and, with much indignation, tells us they are from his village.

Bcharre is famous for its apples and, clearing the ridge, we find ourselves in an orchard in full blossom. From there we head toward a huge oak, our landmark for the tiny church of *Mar Giryes*. Perched on the edge of the cliff, it has a sweeping view of the valley and surrounding mountains. Beautifully simple and recently restored, the church, built in 1800, is so small that the altar, baptismal font and stone pews are outside.

Walking down Main Street Bcharre, we draw curious looks, and Chamoun takes the opportunity to get more signatures for the petition.

It appears the people of Bcharre have an affinity for VW Beetles. On our short walk to the town square we see at least ten, varying from the customized to the dilapidated. As was the

Previous Pages:
> BQARQACHA, ACROSS THE VALLEY
Opposite:
> CLIMBING UP TO BSHARRE FROM THE QADISHA VALLEY
Below:
> FAREED RAHMEH, BCHARRE
> LMT TRAIL BLAZE
> VILLAGE IN WADI QANNOUBINE

case with most mountain towns, many people who chose to emigrate did so to the same country. For the people of Bcharre, it was Australia. I spot the Kangaroo Supermarket. Joe Rahme[19] also is there to greet us and invites us to dinner on behalf of the municipality.

We stop at the Monastery of Mar Sarkis, perched on a steep hillside with a sweeping view of the valley below. It is now the Khalil Gibran Museum and its hermitage houses his tomb. I peer out at the valley and towering mountains and get a glimpse of what must have certainly been a source of inspiration. Mostly known as a writer, Gibran was also a prolific artist and 440 of his works are on display.

The fog rolls in as we head on up to Arz El Rob, or Cedars of the Lord. We pass a conical Phoenician burial site close to the Mzaar of Our Lady of Lourdes, a fascinating reminder of how cultures and religions overlap in so many archeological sites.

The snowline brings with it an unmistakable chill and the group hikes closer as the fog thickens. I am glad we have an experienced guide like Tony, because by the time we reach the hotel, we are in a total white-out and could have easily missed its veiled silhouette.

Later, Sultan drives us into town. Most of us head to the local internet café which, with its Arabic music and Jesus screen savers, has a unique ambience. I can't really say I have missed not having internet for a week.

Previous pages:
> LOOKING DOWN THE WADI QADISHA
Below:
> YOUSSEF, BCHARRE EL ARZ
Opposite:
> ... AND HIS GOATS

Joe Rahme and his wife Aline[20] meet us for dinner at the Sab-bagh restaurant. Aline's father, Youssef Tawk, a conservation-ist, has singlehandedly undertaken significant reforestation projects, even buying plots of land for the sole purpose of re-foresting. Most of the people in the area think he is mad. In their eyes, the cedars are not a cash crop.

The deputy head of the municipality talks to us about environ-mental and ecological issues and is hopeful that the LMT will generate much needed awareness.

By the time we get back to the hotel, the fog has lifted and we decide to take a night hike, hoping it will do our bellies, bulging from the mezze, some good. Light from the full moon reflects off the snow illuminating the whole area, and I am reminded of James Taylor's 'Up on a Roof:' "And at night, the stars, they put on a show for free." It is magical but the biting cold gets the bet-ter of us. Lise-Lotte and I hurry back to the warmth of the hotel.

------------------------
[19] The owner of Eco-Lodge, he and his family are staunch conservationists. He hiked a portion of the LMT in 2007 with Padre and Lise-Lotte.
[20] Aline Tawk is a journalist and follows her father's staunch preservation ideals.

"It is not so much for its beauty that the forest makes a claim upon men's hearts, as for that subtle something, that quality of air, that emanation from old trees, that so wonderfully changes and renews a weary spirit"

ROBERT LOUIS STEVENSON

الأرز إلى حصرون

# The Cedars to Hasroun
## Day 9

Partly sunny blue skies raise our spirits and we think we have dodged the rain that is forecast. The fresh blanket of snow contrasts with the dark green of the cedars, making them even more stunning and majestic. We enter the forest of Arz el Rab with a hushed reverence as if not to disturb their ancient souls. It is quite a feat to be one of the oldest living things on the planet. The trail is hidden beneath the snow and we are careful not to tread on the fragile and precious saplings.

It is believed that there was one continuous cedar mantle that extended the length of the Mount Lebanon chain and beyond into Syria and Turkey. Today, only a few clusters remain, most of which are in preserved areas. Reforestation efforts, often by private individuals, continue, but a lot more needs to be done to protect and preserve our national symbol.

Heading out from the forest we encounter patches of thick mud between the snowfields. We try hopelessly to clean off the mud as it builds up, but finally we just give in to its magnetic attraction to our boots. It is like hiking with weights. To make matters worse, the deep soft snow often gives way unpredictably and

we are plunged thigh-high into its coldness. It is funny for the first half hour. And then, just as we are getting really fed up with the mud, we come to an astounding view of the cedar basin and its cirque[21] of towering peaks. A privileged view that is accessible only by foot. So what's a little mud and snow?

At over 1,900m, the lake of Bqaa Kafra is encircled by snow and looks like a small glacier. Below us are the red tile roofs of the village of Bqaa Kafra[22], the highest in Lebanon. Clouds roll up the mountainside bringing with them a light and erratic drizzle. Understandably, lunch is a wet affair, eaten by an old stone spring. Unlike other orchards we have already passed,

the apple and cherry orchards here are still bare. Spring comes
late at this altitude.

A long and winding road leads us down to the beautiful red-
roofed village of Hasroun, where members of the municipality
welcome us. They have prepared a special 'LMT cake,' which,
along with the hot tea, really hits the spot. It is very encouraging to hear their enthusiasm and commitment to preserving
the trail and footpaths in general. I hope that more municipali-
ties will follow their example. The street to the adjacent town
of Bazaoun is lined with old homes and shops unspoiled by

modern construction. Hotel Karam is a traditional home that has been converted into a guesthouse that has been in the family for over 80 years.

The bus with our weekend hikers arrives before dinner. Bassem is on board as is Norbert's friend, Dana. A Cairo-based photographer and videographer, she is doing a short video on the thru-walk for Time.com. Dana has the ease in manner that comes with experience from being in unfamiliar and perhaps uncomfortable situations.

It is Good Friday and after dinner, Mr. Karam treats us to their homemade *maamoul*. We all gather in the big living room, and the Abou Abed[23] jokes start. Bassem and I retire, but I can still hear clicking glasses. I have a feeling that Dana can probably out-drink Norbert.

------------------------

[21] A bowl-shaped, steep-walled mountain basin carved by glaciation.
[22] Hometown of Mar Charbel, probably the most venerated Lebanese saint.
[23] A national figure of fun, he is the source and butt of Lebanese jokes.

Mount Lebanon

"I love land mines"

حصرون إلى تنورين
## Hasroun to Tannourine
Day 10

George fills in for Sultan for the next few days and gains instant notoriety for snoring so loudly it can be heard through the walls.

He drives our rather boisterous group up to the trailhead where bright sunshine softens the chill of the early morning breeze. Our "Young Goats," as Norbert fondly calls our group of hikers, channel their energy into bouncing and frolicking up the mountainside.

Terraced orchards give way to a more rugged trail as we near the windy mountain pass, where barbed wire fencing has claimed a white owl, preserved perfectly by the cold. Chamoun holds up the beautiful bird to show its impressive 1.5m wingspan. There should be a law against using this kind of fencing in mountain areas. Wildlife has been elusive so far, and it saddens me that the only owl we spot is a victim of negligence.

We arrive at the Tannourine Cedar Forest Nature Reserve at noon. Marie[24] is waiting for us with a wonderful spread of seasonal fruits and vegetables. The rangers have organized a special lunch for us in the shade of a large cedar. They have set up

Previous page:
> WADI RAS BNAYYA
Below:
> ASCENDING  SHIR EL RIBAZ
> THE APPROACH TO THE TANNOURINE RESERVE
> AIN EL DAHAB

a *saj* and prepared the dough for *manakeesh*. Everybody gets into the kneading and baking, making their own "custom" *manousheh*. The scrumptious smell of baking makes it difficult to resist overeating; we still have a long way to go and can't afford to be sluggish. Padre briefed us last night about the grueling climb up Shir[25] el Ribaz.

The ranger briefs us about the reserve and the importance of hiking quietly so as not to disturb the wildlife. Our pace down the snowy slopes of the forest is, however, quite fast. Looking at the mountains across the valley, I notice one mountain that stands out from the rest. Unlike its neighbors, it is totally forested. I ask Lise-Lotte if it's a preserved area. "No," she smiles. "Nobody dares go there because it is littered with land mines from the civil war." It's ironic that the mines, instruments

> TRAIL #1 IN TANNOURINE RESERVE
> *HYPECOUM IMBERBE* SIBTH. AND SM.

"What I see in nature is a magnificent structure that we can comprehend only very imperfectly, and that must fill a thinking person with a feeling of humility. This is a genuinely religious feeling that has nothing to do with mysticism"

ALBERT EINSTEIN

تنورين إلى العاقورة

# Tannourine to Aqoura

## Day 11

The first part of our hike will be along the valley of Nahr el Jawz, named for the large walnut trees that line the valley. We cross an old stone bridge to a water mill surrounded by poplars that George says was still in use 40 years ago.

Most of the trail is on water canals, but there are some parts where recent rockslides have left tricky unstable footing. Lise-Lotte takes a fall that is so bad Padre's face turns white. No broken bones, *hamdillah*. She dusts herself off and jokes about the "technicolor thighs" she's going to have tonight.

We leave the valley and head up toward the village of Chatine with its beautifully-maintained old homes. As we clear the hill, the scenery changes dramatically to a rocky, almost lunar land-scape with weird and wonderful creatures. In the bizarre out-croppings, I can make out a griffin, a dragon and one towering monster standing sentinel over the unlikely pear or-chard that was somehow squeezed in among the rocks.

The thing about sinkholes is that you don't see them coming. A rather ordinary marked footpath takes you down a depression

Previous pages:
> OLD BRIDGE AND WATER MILL, TANNOURINE
AL FAWQA
Below:
> JOSIANNE'S WARM MOUNTAIN WELCOME
> SILENE
Opposite:
> NAHR EL JAWZ

and then you turn a corner and there it is! The huge 255m deep, 25m wide *baatara,* or sinkhole. It is not just its sheer scale that has everyone standing in inarticulate wonder, but the three natural bridges in the foreground of a forceful yet lace-like waterfall plummeting to the depths of the hole. The locals call it *ballouaa* or siphon. I think about what miraculous and unique set of geological conditions came together to form this natural wonder. Fortunately, the Ministry of Environment recently designated the pothole, and a 200m radius around it, a protected area.

To get to our lunch spot at Nabaa el Sheikh we have to walk on a long ledge under a massive cliff face. I hope whatever creatures – I suspect bats – have left the coat of droppings are out to lunch.

Previous pages:
> BAATARA SINKHOLE
Below:
> FATHER MICHEL AND HIS *ABAREEQ*
> BAATARA WATERFALL
> JABAL ARA'EEF IN THE BACKGROUND

The spring gushes out from a tall deep fissure in the rock face. It is ice cold and sweet. The hillside here is so steep that most of us are more leaning against it rather than sitting on it.

We bushwhack up the hill to Laqlouq, where we stop at the Monastery of Deir el Saleeb. The monks come out and offer us water in *Ibreeqs* and invite us inside. We decline because of our sorry muddy state, but we are cheered when, in the distance, we get our first glimpse of a heavily snow-capped Mount Sannine. It is the first time that I have seen its massive profile from the northeast.

It is a long, steep windy downhill to the village of Aqoura. Sporadic rain showers hasten our pace. I look back to see where Bassem and Lise-Lotte are. Not wanting to stop, I keep walking backward… right into a ditch. My legs go up and I start to roll. Were it not for my backpack breaking the momentum, I would have rolled passed everyone right into Aqoura!

If the ratio of churches to population is an indication of religious dedication, then this small village with its 42 churches is definitely the most pious in the country. We are greeted with puzzled smiles and a few flirtatious glances directed mainly at our blue-eyed *ajeneb*.

At the Hassan El-Hachem guesthouse, we meet Trey, who will be joining us for five days. He goes in to town on a quest for a hat. I find it quite adventurous for somebody who's never been to the Middle East. Squeaky clean after our showers by candlelight, we head to dinner at the home of Hassan's mother, Mariam.

Easter Sunday is a festive time here and as soon as we enter the living room they ask, "Beer, whisky, arak, or wine?" Without skipping a beat Norbert answers, "All." Josianne, a well-endowed and very friendly college student, is particularly attentive to Norbert. Our laughter draws in many neighbors. Josianne and Mariam's daughter bring in a variety of piping hot dishes while our seats on the low *diwan* provide interesting vantage points of Josianne's low-cut neckline.

We notice a rather sour-faced little old lady in black sitting in the back. *Teta* Badwannia is Mariam's mother and her name is Turkish, a throwback to the Ottoman period, when Turkish names were given often as a gesture of appeasement. We coax her to sit with us and soon, the camera-shy *Teta* is posing for Norbert while her two rosy-cheeked great-granddaughters look on and giggle themselves silly.

Hassan finally joins us. He says he has been tending to the chickens. At this hour? Mariam explains that the custom on Easter Sunday is for the men to spend the day in the forest, feasting on freshly slaughtered lamb, accompanied with a generous supply of whisky. This explains Hassan's "relaxed" demeanor.

The delicious but rich dinner leaves us feeling heavy and the steep walk back to the guesthouse in the brisk night air does us good. A self-proclaimed computer geek, Trey is very happy that I have a BlackBerry he can use to 'Tweet.' Most of us have never heard of Twitter and decide that will be his nickname. We turn on the heaters and hope our socks will dry.

*"The mountain held the town as in a shadow"*

ROBERT FROST, *The Mountain*

العاقورة إلى أفقا

# Aqoura to Afqa

Day 12

The clear skies that made the night so cold are china blue and an unblinking sun shines down on the expanse of snowfields ahead. This is not what Twitter expected when he planned his springtime hike in the Middle East.

We fill our bottles at the spring of Ain Asafir and commence our hike up the mountain at Sahlet el Jameh, where a blanket of snow softens the rugged highland landscape. We come across a solitary trail of wolf tracks leading up to a distant ridge. This type of hiking can be tricky, and as I look down to watch my step, something bright red catches my attention: ladybugs! Like flitting rubies in the pristine snow. Without a tree or shrub in sight, it is amazing to find them here.

Previous pages:
> AQOURA
> ANEMONE
Below:
> AIN HAROUN
Opposite:
> VIEW OF NAHR IBRAHIM VALLEY FROM JABAL SEHTA
> SEHTA'S SNOWFIELDS
> CUTE BUT TOUGH

It takes us almost three hours to get to the cliffside shrine of
Saydet Sehta. Every year on August 15, scores of the faithful
come to this shrine on foot or by four-wheel drive for the fest
of the Virgin Mary, or *Eid el Saydeh,* to hold an evening mass
and light a bonfire.

Further down along the cliff rim, we reach our panoramic
lunch spot. The view is spectacular. We can see beyond
Laqlouq to the north, the Nahr Ibrahim valley and Mount Sannine to the south. Quietly nibbling on our snacks, our gaze
drifts from cascading waterfalls, turquoise lakes and gushing
rivers to green mountain slopes, arid highlands and snow-
capped summits.

Far below, nestled on the side of the mountain, is Aqoura. It looks
so peaceful from here, but we know better. Mariam is probably
bossing everyone around with the chores. Josianne, slightly disappointed by a rather unfruitful evening, goes back to her second
priority, college. And Hassan is still sleeping off his hangover.

As we begin our descent of Mount Sehta, we leave its snowfields behind. We have been on the snow for over four hours
and now we hike through bright green meadows with clusters
of white-blossomed *Khokh el Dib*[26] trees. This mountain has
one of the largest juniper forests in Lebanon.

Charred skeletal trees bear testament to the forest fire, caused
by human negligence, that ravaged a large area of the mountain
in 1997. Skirting around the beautifully wooded hill of Mnaitra,
we see the ruins of its Crusader fort and the commanding view
it offered those it once protected.

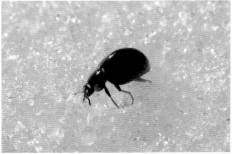

Close to the entrance of La Reserve[27] we run into Boutros Asaker and his 400 goats. He tells us how every spring around mid-May he takes the entire herd up to the Sehta highlands, where they stay till the end of summer. Most goat herders do this to escape the heat and avoid exhausting the grazing grounds. By this time, the kids are weaned and the nanny goats are ready for milking. It is the season for making *shankleesh*, the cheese *mezze* served with oil and spices.

The parking lot seems unreasonably far from our cabin. Even though I am hot, tired and have an upset stomach, I decide not to complain. Chamoun and Twitter, seeing my pathetic attempts to carry my first bag, come to my aid. I crash on my bunk, trying not to think about how I am going to schlep the other bags back up the hill. I thank them from the bottom of my heart. We all really need tomorrow's rest day, except Twitter maybe. He has so much energy he'll probably go climb some cliff or something. He has been going "off-road," taking side trips from the trail all day and probably covered twice the distance we did.

While lying alone in the cabin I notice an almost imperceptible movement in the corner. I lie perfectly still and then it moves again, this time scurrying boldly across the room: a field mouse. After having assessed the solid inventory of goodies in our bags, I presume it's going back to tell his buddies it'll be party time tonight.

------------------------

[26] Bear Plum, *Prunus ursina.*
[27] La Reserve of Afqa: a camp offering many activities, such as climbing courses and summer camp for youth groups.

*"Truly it may be said that the outside of a mountain is good for the inside of a man"*

GEORGE WHERRY, *Alpine Notes and the Climbing Foot*

أفقا

# Afqa - Rest day

## Day 13

I sleep well and wake up feeling much better.

The Afqa region, with its cliffs, is an ideal location for rock climbing courses, and at breakfast there is much bustle as a group of around 40 students gets ready for a day on the rocks. A few look as if they know what they are doing while others appear clueless. We meet Henri, the French climbing instructor. He first came to Lebanon as a soldier with the United Nations in 1982 and loved the country so much he decided to come back. Since his return, he has been teaching climbing to, among others, the Lebanese army's Special Forces.

I have often tried to identify and define the intangible pull this country has on foreigners that draws them back to stay, despite the political instability. Is it the temperate climate, the unique cultural mix, natural beauty, rich history and heritage, or the palpable energy coursing through the country?

The climbers leave and we are quite happy to have the place to ourselves. We have long hot showers courtesy of the solar water heaters and hang a week's laundry on juniper bushes and guy wires. It's nice not to be moving for a change. To be able to just sit back and take in the scenery. There is outdoor music courtesy of Twitter's iPod. He takes our requests from the Gypsy Kings to Bach, although we are not quite as perky as we were on our last rest day; nobody even suggests going for a walk.

We have a lot of "admin" to catch up on: Padre has the trip logistics, Norbert organizes his photographs, Lise-Lotte with her GPS coordinates and I am busy with my diary writing. It is not so much that we are physically fatigued or that the size of the walk is overwhelming, but sometimes you simply need a break.

Wim has been eying the flimsy tarp covering the cabin with disapproval. He doesn't believe it can withstand rain and wind and decides to try and secure it more firmly with the help of Marathon Man and Twitter. When they are done, he is still skeptical, especially since showers are forecast for tonight.

Vasso comes to visit in the afternoon carrying a bottle of wine and nuts. Sitting lazily on the grass, we watch the sun set over the hazy valley. High above, a couple of hawks are riding the air currents looking for field mice.

Gray clouds have delivered a cold and windy front. We have dinner in the comfy warmth of the recreation room. My upset stomach is better, but for safe measure, Vasso gives me his mother's old Armenian remedy: a tablespoon of sumac. It's like trying to swallow a mouthful of tart sawdust and involves many forced gulps and two glasses of water to wash it down. I hope it's worth it.

It has already started to drizzle as we head back down the slippery path with only the narrow beams of our headlamps lighting the way. Falling asleep is easy. Staying asleep is another matter. Much to my annoyance, at 11 p.m. the rowdy climbers still haven't settled down. Adding to the cacophony is the sound of multiple retching. Things finally settle down when they have nothing left to throw up.

A more subtle sound wakes me next. Water dripping. It sounds very close, as if it's right near my ear. It is right near my

ear! I feel a wet spot right next to my pillow. I turn on my flashlight and the whole cabin is dripping. Wim was right about the tarp. Padre is moving our stuff quietly in the dark so it doesn't get soaked while the rest sleep blissfully unaware of our wet dilemma. Twitter is the only one sleeping on an upper bunk, so he is on the frontline of the indoor drizzle. Padre tries to wake him to no avail. He finally gets up before dawn, wraps his sopping sleeping bag around him and heads out the door in search of a drier refuge.

"The source of the Adonis waters, where a temple stood... called by the Greeks, Aphaca, the kiss. Here Adonis and Astarte first loved in legend, and the god hunted and died where the great river flows from the mountain"

COLIN THUBRON, *The Hills of Adonis*

أفقا إلى حراجل

# Afqa to Hrajel

## Day 14

There will be an abundance of springs and water sources on the way to Hrajel today. We put on our best raingear but, as we head out into the light but steady rain, I sense that lack of water is going to be the least of our worries.

At Ain el Hosn, we cross to the other side of the valley. Through the shifting clouds, we get glimpses of a dramatic landscape of rock formations, overhangs, cliffs and caves. Clearing the mountain pass, we are met with a strong headwind that further challenges our strained progress. The torrential river below foretells its source, the Afqa Cave.

The entrance to the colossal cave is imposing. The more energetic among us venture up to peer into its gaping blackness. They appear now as minute specks and define its scale. The deafening roar of the powerful cascade forces us to communicate in signs. The entire side of the mountain seems about to burst, with water coming out of every pore and crevice. The vastness of the cave and its powerful waterfall are both humbling and moving. I know that my goose bumps are not because of the cold. I turn to Lise-Lotte to try and say something and find that I am choked up. Over a waterfall!

Previous pages:
> THE ADONIS RIVER
> SHIR EL GHARIB AS SEEN FROM THE CABIN IN
AFQA RESERVE

Across the old stone bridge are the ruins of the Temple of Venus. In his quest for the cult of Adonis, the British travel writer, Colin Thubron, visited and explored many sites all over Lebanon. The Astarte[28] temple of Afqa is one of the most significant because it is here that the myth of Adonis and Astarte was born.

## A STORY OF TRAGIC LOVE AND DEATH

In classical Greek mythology, Apheca is associated with the cult of Aphrodite and Adonis. According to the myth, Cinyras, the King of Cyprus, seduced his daughter, Myrra, who was transformed into a tree that bears her name. After several months, the tree split open and the child Adonis emerged. He was reared by Aphrodite, who became enamored of him,

causing her lover, Ares, to become jealous. Ares sent a vicious boar to kill Adonis, and, at the pool at the foot of the falls of Apheca, Adonis bled to death from a deep wound in the groin. Aphrodite despaired at his death and out of pity for her the gods allowed Adonis to ascend from the underworld for a short period each year.

Each spring at Apheca, the melting snows flood the river, bringing a reddish mud into the stream from the steep mountain slopes. The red stain can be seen feeding into the river and far out to the Mediterranean Sea. Legend held this to be the blood of Adonis, renewed each year at the time of his death, while local legend also has it that the red anemones that bloom in the valley of the Adonis River or Nahr Ibrahim, are tainted with his blood.

We head on up to the cliffs overlooking Lassa, but visibility is poor. We finally seek refuge from the incessant rain in a rather unusual stone refuge higher up on the mountainside. It is around 20m long with 1.5-meter thick walls, and has two doors and a window. Inside, the walls, blackened from wood fires, are bone dry. We guess it must be a shelter for shepherds.

Most of the trail follows a long escarpment, and I am careful not to venture too close to the edge. I would like to avoid ending my ambitious trek prematurely among sharp craggy rocks. Our breaks are now determined by whenever we can find shelter. We happen upon a lonesome one-room hut, still under construction with one invaluable quality: a finished roof. One after another, we stumble clumsily into the small, dry room.

Below:
> NABAA EL QANA
> SHIR EL KISSEH
Next pages:
> GOAT SHELTER NEAR AIN ABBAS

Seven wet hikers, backpacks, and walking sticks, all negotiating cinder blocks and protruding iron rods: such grace and poise. We have had more scenic, pastoral lunches, but none this comical.

The trail now leaves the ridgeline and we cross a plateau to fertile pastures. The quaint church of Saydet Darje sits on a steep hill overlooking the town of Hrajel. Darje in Arabic means steps, and, true to its name, there are steps leading down the hillside towards the town, but they soon become

a vague path of rubble and mud. Circling gracefully above the village is a large flock of migrating storks. Thanks to the foul weather, they escape being used for target practice by local hunters.

The many signs to the magnificently named Smash Mountain Hotel make it quick and easy to find. Joseph Zoughaib and his daughter, Caren, are waiting for us. Recently widowed, he is struggling to keep his business afloat. The hotel is a ski lodge, used mainly by schools and youth groups during the winter and camps in the summer. Spring is off-season and we are the only guests. Our dorm is in what must be the daycare section of the lodge. There is a small hall outside our room where we peel off our wet and muddy clothes. Norbert does a little striptease against a backdrop of brightly painted walls with cartoon characters. His antics in black long johns have us in stitches.

The big kids in our group make use of the games available. Twitter teaches Hollandi *tawla*, or backgammon, while Marathon Man and Nimsawi battle it out in a fierce game of table tennis. I ask Joseph for a heater to dry out my boots and he gets me something far better, a boot dryer. Not being a skier, I didn't even know such a contraption existed. Needless to say, we are all thrilled and take turns using it. It actually works quite well.

Joseph's homemade pizza and salad are just what we were all craving, and we eat far more than we should. We sip his homegrown herbal tea while waiting for the weather forecast. A full-fledged storm will be pounding the country by morning.

------------------------------

[28] Phoenician equivalent to the Roman Venus and the Greek Aphrodite.

"Bury me where I fall with my flag"

حراجل إلى كفر ذبيان

# Hrajel to Kfar Dibiane
## Day 15

As the storm rages outside, we work on being creative. Chamoun's efforts involve several colorful garbage bags and an umbrella – waterproofing techniques, required in light of the previous day's deluge. We then bravely head out, spirits high and humming 'Singing in the Rain.'

Looking down helps prevent the rain from trickling down my neck and focuses my vision on the paved road, on which it looks like somebody has spilled a bowl of noodles. They are, in fact, squirming foot-long earthworms, flushed out by the torrent of the previous night. I shake off my grossed-out feeling and continue trudging along the 5km uphill trail, bent and buffeted by the wind.

Our local guide did not make it today (nothing to do with the weather, I'm sure), so we find ourselves plodding alone into a cold and stinging storm. Padre takes control, following the 'trail blazes' and his map. Even though he and Lise-Lotte are familiar with this section of the LMT, the fog and rain reduce visibility to just a few meters.

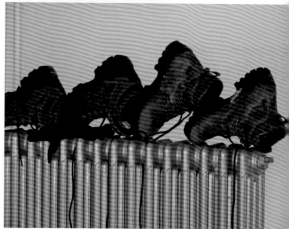

The trail along the canal is supposed to be easy, but instead it is an obstacle course of overgrown brambles and collapsed terrace walls. Dense fog concentrates the eye on a more intimate scale. Coming out of a crack in the canal are a pair of salamanders. Their yellow and black markings are striking against the concrete canal walls.

The thunderclaps get louder, the lightning closer and the rain turns into a stinging sleet. Despite the obvious danger, Chamoun refuses to give up his umbrella and continues walking around like a human lightning rod. He has given instructions to Norbert that, in the event of his spontaneous combustion on the mountain, he is to be buried with his flag where he falls.

Taking cover in an abandoned and leaky shack, only then do we realize how drenched we are. No matter how well dressed you are for the rain, if you are out in it long enough, the wetness will find its way in. Padre is now seriously considering calling it a day. The poor visibility and numerous cliffs are making hiking dangerous. We were all secretly hoping for this, except maybe Marathon Man. My only regret is missing out on seeing the Kfar Dibiane natural bridge[29]. I make a mental note to put it on my places-to-come-back-to list.

Cell phone reception is erratic, making it difficult to communicate with George to arrange a pick up. We brace ourselves and head back out, resigning ourselves to the inevitable frigid wetness. We are still laughing and joking. There is something about being inside a thunderstorm cloud that is strangely energizing.

We are heading down into what Padre tells us is a valley. The swirling fog briefly reveals the large stone columns of the

Roman ruins of Kfar Dibiane. We finally get through to George and hike to a small road to meet him. These back roads aren't even on the map and Josephine, the manager of Auberge Beity in Kfar Dibiane, a youth hostel affiliated to an adjacent convent, had to accompany him to help find us.

The aromas from the kitchen greet us while we thaw out in our rooms. Limp boots, draped with wet woolen socks sit on the radiator. Ponchos, hung out to dry in the bathroom, drip sluggishly. Twitter is in desperate need of warmer clothes and we decide to visit a nearby ski shop, where we all manage to find something to buy. I am doubtful that my sopping boots will recover by tomorrow and I buy a pair of ugly, but comfortable, replacements.

By the time we get back, the youth group staying at the hostel has returned from their excursion. They are taking part in an inter-faith dialogue and bonding weekend. It is heartening to see a scarfed 'Fatima' with a young 'Pierre' and his wooden cross, walking down the hallway laughing together. I believe that the hope for post-civil war rapprochement and mutual trust between the country's different confessions lies in our youth.

Norbert has been challenging Marathon Man to obtain random items from the villagers along the way. I have been curious about the contents of the burlap bag he has been carrying around lately. It looks like wheat. Today, he has risen to the occasion and produced a cake for Lise-Lotte's birthday. We are all very impressed and dig in, reassured that we will be burning it off tomorrow... weather permitting.

------------------------

[29] An extremely rare natural occurrence, this land bridge, a product of hundreds of thousands of years of unique geological conditions, is massive in scale (52m long and 58m in height).

"Of two men looking at a green field, one estimates its yield in bushels and calculates the price of the bushels in silver and in gold. The other drinks the greenness of the field with his eye, and kisses every blade with his thought, and fraternizes in his soul with every rootlet and pebble, and every clod of earth"

MIKHAIL NAIMY

كفر ذبيان إلى بسكنتا

# Kfar Dibiane to Baskinta

## Day 16

*B*y daybreak, the tempest abates slightly. We hope that the brunt of the storm has passed as we get on the bus taking us to the trailhead at Bakish. On our way, we pass the town square of Kfar Aqab. Our guide, Carole Akl, tells me that the square is called *blata*, or slab, bringing to mind the *blata* in Amine Maalouf's fictional town of Kfar Yabda in *The Rock of Tanios*. In fact, Maalouf's hometown is the neighboring village of Ain el Qabou.

Silhouettes of bare trees, soaked dark brown, peep out from the eerie mist. Stubborn blades of grass and vibrant spring blooms push out through the thick layer of hail, as if protesting the unseasonal intrusion. All around there is the soft trickle of water. Towering above us are the imposing cliffs of Shwar Baskinta. These cliffs are part of a long ridgeline that delineates a fault line running, north to south along the western slopes of the Mount Lebanon chain. High above the cliffs is Qanat Bakish, home to one of the oldest of Lebanon's six ski resorts. We are so taken with this spectacularly unusual mountainscape we hardly notice the intermittent drizzle. After the thrashing we got from yesterday's storm, it seems inconsequential.

Previous pages:
> WADI EL MSANN
Opposite:
> *ASPHODELINE LUTEA* (L.) RCHB
Below:
> SNOW MELT
> FLOODED ROAD BELOW SHWAR BASKINTA

Our first destination is the Mikhail Naimy Mausoleum, which marks the starting point of the Baskinta Literary Trail[30]. The arched trees lining the footpath to the tomb are reminiscent of a Cezanne painting and the fresh whiteness of the hail lends it serenity. The stone door to the crypt is slightly ajar, symbolic of Naimy's philosophy that there is no barrier between life and death. There is a statue and the water streaming down his face makes it look like he is weeping.

Mikhail Naimy was born in Baskinta in 1889. Much of the settings and symbolism in his works are inspired by the natural beauty of the area. Like his friend Khalil Gibran, Naimy lived overseas for over 20 years. After Gibran's death in 1932, he returned to his beloved Baskinta, where he lived and wrote till his death in 1988 at the age of 99.

Leaving the Naimy house, we head down a valley and pass by a long row of beehives. Chamoun tells me that there are two kinds of bees in Lebanon: Lebanese and Italian. The Italians, being the

more aggressive, are known to sting even if unprovoked. I keep my distance. Padre pushes back some overgrown bushes and uncovers another stone slab with a Roman inscription.

We are now at the tip of Wadi el Delb. The massive rock walls of the valley narrow, black streaks bleeding down their deeply grooved gray face. We come to a clearing overlooking the valley, a vibrant green meadow and we wade through knee-high grass to the edge of the field.

In the cliff face across the valley is a large cave entrance partially blocked by a stone wall. No one really knows why it is called the Cave of Saif El Dawleh[31]. It is accessible only by ropes and several caving associations have explored it, but how and why it is there remains a mystery.

Below:
> WINTER'S INTRUSION ON SPRING
> TREES IN THE FOG
Next pages:
> ON THE WAY TO SHAKHROUB

The clouds have lifted. Overhead, three storks appear lost. Disoriented by the storm, they must have been separated from their flock. One of them leaves the rest and circles slowly down with effortless grace. The large black and white bird with scarlet legs and bill alights at a nearby spring. An elegant visitor, it is stranded here by a storm that has perhaps saved its life. Hunters don't care much for stormy weather.

We stop for lunch at the red-roofed church of Saydet el Khalleh, sitting in a large field of daisies. The cold sets in as soon as we stop moving, and we hurry through the meal. I put on my gloves before my hands become too numb to grasp my walking sticks. After negotiating several slick and tricky stream crossings, we finally commence our descent into the wonderfully-named Wadi Jamajim, or Valley of the Skulls.

The meter-wide stone path leading in and out of the valley is Roman, as is the bridge crossing the river. Romans, Romans everywhere. It has withstood the torrential springtime river for thousands of years. Those Romans sure knew how to build.

When we clear the crest, we find ourselves on the outskirts of Baskinta. It is one of the few Lebanese villages that, due to local preservation efforts, has retained its original identity, unadulterated by modern construction and "improvements."

The Khoury Hanna guesthouse is a typical Lebanese mountain home: a rectangular floor plan, stone walls, red tile roof and *mandaloun* arches. Our hostess, Michelle, is the great grand daughter of Ibrahim Khoury el Hanna, who built this house in 1878. Jean Aroyan, Michelle's husband, tells us how the young Ibrahim fell in love with the daughter of Emir Youssef Fandi Abillama, Badr el Muna. The Emir was against the union, considering Ibrahim not

Below:
> *ANTHEMIS CHIA* L.
> RUINS OF A HOUSE IN EL KHALLEH AREA
Opposite:
> RIVER CROSSING IN WADI EL KHALLEH

good enough for his daughter. Undeterred, our hero immigrated to the US vowing to make his fortune, while his beloved promised to wait. Years later, and flush with cash – he is in fact richer than his future father-in-law – he returns to claim his bride.

The "weekenders" arrive shortly after we settle in. I notice that it is a larger group this time, and have a feeling the weekend groups will be getting bigger as the trip progresses. I am very excited that Hadi[32] has come with Bassem for the weekend. The staff at my gym have sent me a basket of goodies with my favorite cupcakes and a note saying how proud they are. Lise-Lotte is under the weather, and after dinner Norbert fixes her a hot toddy, a warm beverage with a nip of alcohol. We kick out the non-essential personnel from the room so she can sleep. Hadi and I have a lot of catching up to do, and we exchange whispers by the light of the *sobia.*

------------------------

[30] The BLT is an optional side trail of the LMT. The 24km trail visits 22 literary landmarks related to several acclaimed poets and novelists from the region, including Mikhail Naimy, Amin Maalouf, Abdallah Ghanem, Suleiman Kettaneh, Rachid Ayoub and Georges Ghanem.
[31] The Sword of the Nation.
[32] Hana's youngest son.

"Nature grows desolate without history, like a bone without flesh; but wherever paths cross the countryside assumes memories and is invisibly softened. The whole of Lebanon falls within this vale of recollection. There cannot be a knoll which is free from the past"

COLIN THUBRON, *The Hills of Adonis*

بسكنتا إلى المتين
# Baskinta to Mtain
## Day 17

Sultan is back and I also discover that he is a magician. With his special talent he fits all 24 of us with our luggage and backpacks into the bus. We will be re-joining the LMT at the Naimy tomb. Sultan negotiates the narrow icy road with skill and confidence. The excess weight is at least good for traction.

The brief morning sun reveals our first view of the majestic white slopes of Sannine. Clouds roll up from the valleys and soon cover the mountain and turn the sky slate gray. We had hoped for more sunshine this morning.

Heading west along the flanks of the mountain, we come to a sweeping hilltop with clusters of rubble scattered throughout. Pierre, our guide, tells us we are looking at the ruins of a Roman town. The large stone portal of the temple has cobra carvings, indicating it might date back to Phoenician times.

When Pierre first started hiking to this spot as a young boy, there used to be twelve Greek or Roman sarcophagi at the site. Looters have taken nine as well as most of the walls of the buildings. A huge walnut tree stands out among the flattened

ruins. Its gnarled and hollowed out trunk was a holy site for
the different civilizations that passed through. The large stone
slab engraved with crusader crosses that used to lie near the
tree is gone, also claimed by looters. I leave the site both in-
trigued and heavy hearted.

We come to a remarkable gorge, where the river, over time,
has smoothed the rock into soft undulating curves, creating
large pools of swirling water. To our right, we catch glimpses
of the towns and villages of Mrouj, Khenshara, Jouar, Dhour
Shoueir and Bikfaya, all below us. Lunch is atop a maze of pe-
culiar outcroppings. The 3m high pillar-like structures are flat
on top and very comfortable.

After climbing several small hills, we get our first view of Jabal
Knaisseh, or Mountain of the Small Church. It is rather odd
that even though it is around the same elevation as Sannine,
there is no snow[33]. I guess the storm decided to concentrate
its force on a group of seven hikers on Sannine.

The town of Mtain is now visible, hugging the mountainside overlooking Wadi Salima. The trail seems to have blended and disappeared into the terraced slopes and we resort to bushwhacking the rest of the way to town.

We are greeted, not by our hosts or friendly townspeople, but by the pungent smell of arak and winemaking. Joseph Khairallah is the owner of this small winery and distillery. He and his son give us a tour of stills, vats, and barrels.

They produce arak, wine and even whisky. Lebanese whisky? Norbert confirms that there is in fact such a thing. It does not take any arm twisting for Joseph to pose with a glass of wine,

especially when he finds out about Norbert's wine book. Joseph and his son open a bottle of their wine and suddenly it's "Happy Hour." The vapors alone have already left me a bit light-headed, much to Norbert's amusement. I leave him and Joseph discussing the finer points of winemaking and head back into the fresh air and on to the 400-year-old Qontar Guesthouse.

The outer walls of the house are on the town square. The deep arched entrance leads to an inner courtyard with blossom trees and large pots overflowing with a spring palette of blooms. Faisal Qontar and his sisters, Leila and Nejiba, welcome us with homemade lemonade.

Faisal Abu-Izzeddine[34] gives us a tour of Mtain's newly renovated town square, one of the success stories of the LMT project. Faisal's efforts, and those of the mayor, Zouheir Abi Nader, who believed in the project and fought for it despite intense opposition, deserve recognition. It has recaptured the beauty and character of the central point of the town. But many of the stores remain empty. Hopefully more hiking groups and tourists coming through this charming town will breathe life back into it.

Previous pages:
> NAHR MICHMICHE
Opposite:
> AFTER THE RIVER CROSSING
Below:
> QONTAR GUESTHOUSE ENTRANCE, MTAIN
> VIEW OF SHIR NSOUR IN QANAT BAKISH

Bassem is not thrilled about the segregated sleeping arrangements, but we respect the house rules. The ladies' "dorm" is on the upper level, overlooking the courtyard. It is also the living room where Leila and Nejiba receive a steady stream of visitors. It is impressive how they juggle being hosts while preparing dinner for 24 hungry hikers.

In the spacious vaulted dining room, they bring out, among other dishes, *burghol bi dfeen* on large pewter platters that are family heirlooms. Everything on the table is homemade and homegrown. Among the many preserves they have for dessert is the best grape molasses I have ever tasted. I plead with them to sell me some but they have to save their limited supply for guests. I will have to wait for the next batch in the fall.

[33] Mount Knaisseh is in fact lower than Mount Sannine, hence the lack of snow. The elevation was deceptive from where the author was standing.
[34] Project manager of the USAID-funded LMT Project (Dec 2005 – Mar 2008).

"Breathes there the man, with soul so dead,
Who never to himself has said,
This is my own, my native land"

SIR WALTER SCOTT, *The Lay of the Last Minstrel*

المتين إلى فالوغا

# Mtain to Falougha
## Day 18

Nejiba and Leila are already making wholegrain *saj manakeesh* and large, steaming pots of foul are already on the table when we come down for breakfast. We eat and, in what is now a familiar routine, set off.

On the outskirts of the village we pass the roofless ruins of a large silk factory, a vestige of Lebanon's thriving silk industry. In the 18th century, Lebanon had already begun to specialize in raw silk production, but by the 19th century the industry had grown so much that half of Mount Lebanon's population depended on it. In fact, the heaviest period of immigration followed the collapse of the silk industry in Lebanon in 1912.

Further down the path, our guide, Joseph Lteif, points out the stone wheel and channeled trough of a grape press. Perhaps Leila and Nejiba's ancestors perfected the art of grape molasses making here? We begin our descent to the valley of Nahr Rmeil. Joseph informs us that the well-preserved cobbled byway is an Ottoman carriage road. The waterfall near the bridge (also Ottoman) refreshes us with a light, cold spray. Behind and around the waterfall is a plush wall of ferns and moss.

Our long steep ascent to Qornayel is in the shade of a forest of umbrella pines (a.k.a. stone pine)[35]. A tapestry of pastel blooms covers the forest floor: cyclamens, daisies and anemones.

Our arrival is met with villagers marking their territory: a display of screeching tires and handbrake turns from an old Mercedes. I am impressed that a group of unassuming and weary hikers could provoke such a reaction. Some villagers are still suspicious of strangers passing through their town. The encounter ends uneventfully and we continue on our way through the settling dust.

Walking along the wooded spine of the mountain, we look back at Sannine. It is hard to believe that only four days ago we were on the other side of this mountain. Up ahead is Jabal Knaisseh, to the south Barouk and Mount Hermon, three of the highest peaks in Lebanon. To the west, we see a small sliver of Rafik Hariri International Airport with the Mediterranean peeping out between hazy blue mountains.

We meet a goatherd with his three dogs and a mule taking the flock to their summer residence in the *jurd* of Knaisseh.

We walk through the middle of the herd, the animals sashaying nimbly past us with the dogs keeping them all in line.

The trail meanders between recently excavated irrigation ponds up to the famous Ain el Saha spring. From here we contour along the western slopes of the mountain and notice in the distance a dark green hilltop overlooking Falougha. Tallet el Alam, or Hilltop of the Flag, is another example of a private reforestation initiative. In 1932, Bahije Merhij, from Falougha, began planting the hill with cedars, a project that took several years. This is also the site where the first Lebanese flag was raised in 1943 to mark Lebanon's independence, hence the name.

Tareq Halabi and his father are waiting for us on the terrace of their summer home. Twitter reluctantly leaves with the weekenders, his preconception of Lebanon turned on its head in the space of a week. He half-jokingly asks how hard it is to get a job in Lebanon. We will miss him. Meanwhile, Chamoun will be spending the next two nights in his nearby hometown of Chbainieh.

Abu Tareq loves to cook, but what he loves even more is feeding his guests. When Chamoun pops in for a surprise visit with a box full of pastries, I can't believe we actually find room for them in our bulging bellies. These are very special cakes because Chamoun actually paid for them. His no-money principle apparently doesn't apply in his hometown.

The Halabis spend the winter months in their apartment in Beirut. Tareq, a proud new father, is anxious to get back to his baby boy. They leave us in the care of their helper and will return in the morning for breakfast. We gather round the wood burning stove in the living room full, warm, content and chatting away until drowsiness overtakes us.

------------------------

[35] *Pinus pinea*. Species of pine native to Southern Europe, North Africa and the Levant.

"Your living is determined not so much by what life brings to you as by the attitude you bring to life; not so much by what happens to you as by the way your mind looks at what happens"

KHALIL GIBRAN

فالوغا

# Falougha - Rest day

Day 19

In the morning, dawn is only just leaking in as Lise-Lotte and I sit at the dining room table sipping our coffees, writing, chatting and enjoying some quiet time together. These moments will be few and far between from now on. Florian, a Frenchman, will be joining us tomorrow morning, and two photojournalists from Milan will meet us in Ain Zhalta. Abu Tareq is back at 8 a.m. and covers the table with a large assortment of homemade foods, the most exceptional being his honey. Among other things, Abu Tareq was a beekeeper for over 30 years.

In the course of our conversations, I also discover he has a talent for quoting poetry and prose with impeccable timing. He is also known for being a notorious thorn in the side of the town's municipality and potential "developers," staunchly opposing illegal construction projects and environmental abuse.

My family comes to join us for lunch. I haven't seen my mom in three weeks and she is reassured to see me looking healthy. She still doesn't know about my sick days in Akkar. It hasn't been easy for my over-protective mom to have a daughter with a penchant for adventure. When we returned from Tanzania,

I found out that her blood pressure had skyrocketed the whole time we were climbing Kilimanjaro. She still drops hints that maybe I could have more "normal" pursuits, but is supportive when her efforts to dissuade me inevitably fail.

We have a gloriously lazy afternoon and watch the sunset over the Lamartine Valley (a.k.a. the Valley of Nahr Beirut). In 1835, the French poet Alphonse de Lamartine visited Lebanon. Many of the sites that he stayed at bear his name. Known as 'the poet of meditations,' the Lebanese mountains seem to have inspired him as they did Gibran and Naimy.

"Everything is blooming most recklessly; if it were voices instead of colors, there would be an unbelievable shrieking into the heart of the night"

RAINER MARIA RILKE

فالوغا إلى عين زحلتا

# Falougha to Ain Zhalta
## Day 20

Breakfast is a big steaming pot of Abu Tareq's *kishk*. Nobody is really hungry, but saying no is not an option. Just before leaving, he takes me to his pantry and gives me two jars of his precious honey.

On the way to the trailhead at Tallet el Alam, we spot an eagle, regally perched on a tree not far from the road. Unperturbed by our presence, it remains on its branch, as if posing for the thrilled photographers.

The large basin we hike through is dotted with trenches and ditches. This used to be a strategic position for the Syrian artillery. Today, the Lebanese army uses it for summer military exercises, while Marathon Man uses it for his training: running up and down the rocky slopes with tires tied to his waist. He tells me it's one of his favorite things to do. I tell him he's mad.

There is an elaborate tunnel system that leads to an underground military hospital that the French built during World War II. We are told we need special permission to visit, so we will have to return another time.

Previous pages:
> CHERRY BLOSSOMS
> LOOKING UP INTO THE CANOPY OF THE APTLY
NAMED UMBRELLA PINES
Below:
> FLOWER CONFETTI HEALING THE SCARS OF CONFLICT
> YOUSSEF "TWO STICKS" ZEITOUNI, AIN DARA
Opposite:
> CHERRY TREE

As we clear the cusp of the basin, we get our first view of the Beqaa Valley steeped in a smoky mid-morning mist. At the end of the downhill trail is the Beirut-Damascus highway and the Dahr el Baydar checkpoint. The internal Security Forces are very curious, not to mention quite impressed, about our journey. One of the officers says he would like to join us all the way to Marjaayoun… if only he had the time.

It is so strange to be crossing Dahr el Baydar from North to South. Even though we passed our halfway point a few days ago, for me this is a more meaningful milestone. I can better visualize our progress by relating it to a familiar landmark.

We share a dirt road with a constant stream of trucks laden with pieces of a mountain that is being ravaged and torn down. We stare helplessly at the ever-increasing gaping wound. There are laws and restrictions against quarries in Lebanon, but some are clearly above the law.

The trail winds between softly rolling hills. There are wildflowers in dazzling profusion, blossoming from every twig and carpeting every sunny slope. The big ditches in which Syrian tanks used to sit are filled with the confetti of flowers, the color of Easter eggs. Nature is healing the scars of conflict.

The village of Ain Dara is known for the battle of 1711 that marked a shift in the allegiance of two branches of the Druze, the Yemenis and the Qaysis. Today, the town is a picture of tranquility. We stop at the town square where Lise-Lotte buys ice cream. We follow suit. I can't remember when I last had ice cream. Curious but friendly townspeople gather round and Chamoun gets a few more signatures on the petition.

Shortly after leaving the town, we meet a farmer in one of the many surrounding orchards. Youssef Zeitouni uses two walking sticks because his knees are bad. He brandishes the sharply tapered one that he has used to kill many snakes. Seeing the look of alarm and dread on my face, Youssef "Two Sticks" reassures me that if you make enough noise while hiking, snakes will usually avoid you. So much for hiking quietly so as not to disturb the wildlife.

After a long and sweaty uphill trek in the sun, we are grateful for the shade of the umbrella pines at our lunch spot. Lying sprawled on a cushion of pine needles, Padre treats us to some pomelos that he bought in Ain Dara. Why would something as mundane as a pomelo seem like a treat? Hiking, especially for a long time, makes you appreciate all the small things in life that we city folk take for granted: running water, hot showers, ice cream, air conditioning, toilets, electricity… and pomelos.

More uphill. The landscape is becoming more rugged and we can now see the wooded slopes of the northernmost portion of the Chouf Cedar Reserve. To the south, and at the foothills

of the Barouk Mountains, is Ain Zhalta. The downhill approach gives us a broad view of the area and the neighboring villages of Bmahray and Nabaa es Safa.

The Hotel Victoria sits on a knoll in the middle of a cedar grove. A shadow of its former glory, bordering on dilapidation, it now serves as a guesthouse for school groups and hikers. In its day, it used to be a resort hotel for actors, artists and the jet set.

The first thing on everyone's mind is a shower. The good news is that the showers are hot, the beds clean and comfortable and the view from our windows beautiful. We also have tons of room and privacy. Vasso has brought a bag of freshly picked *foul* pods, and we sit on the entrance steps sunning like lizards and nibble away.

Maurizio and Marco, the Italian photojournalists, arrive in the dark just in time for dinner. They are well prepared and whip out their headlamps. It is ironic that the one day we ask for a spaghetti dinner, the Italians arrive. They will have 10 more days to sample Lebanese mountain cuisine. They are quickly included in Norbert and Wim's nightly ritual of "Scottish tea" drinking.

"For in the true nature of things, if we rightly consider, every green tree is far more glorious than if it were made of gold and silver"

MARTIN LUTHER

عين زحلتا إلى الباروك
# Ain Zhalta to Barouk
## Day 21

Breakfast is in the shade of cedars with *manakeesh* straight from the oven, garden-fresh cucumbers, mint and a brisk breeze. We are ready to go.

We begin our four-day trek through the Chouf Cedar Reserve at the Ain Zhalta-Bmahray entrance. The reserve is home to half of Lebanon's iconic cedars. Several successful reforestation campaigns, by Lebanon's Green Plan in the 1960s and more recently by local NGOs, have reforested large areas of the reserve with cedars and other indigenous trees.

Lise-Lotte has been speaking furtively on the phone all morning. When I ask her what's going she just smiles and says, "It's a surprise." She tells us to go ahead. She will catch up with us shortly.

We begin with a steady 6km climb to the ridgeline. I look back for Lise-Lotte and see her hiking with my "surprise." Michel Moufarege[36] introduced me to hiking in the Lebanese mountains. His passion for the mountains is intense, his wealth of knowledge of them uncanny. I think of him as my "Mountain Muse." He asks me if the trek is living up to my expectations and I tell me him it has surpassed them from the very first day.

The higher elevations bring with them scattered snowfields. By mid-morning we reach the ridge at 1,900m with sweeping views in all directions. San-nine, Knaissseh, the Beqaa, Barouk, Mount Hermon and, in the hazy dis-tance, the Mediterranean.

The track follows the ridgeline for 8km. It is as if we are walking down the back-bone of Lebanon. As we near one of the higher peaks, we traverse a brilliant white scarf of snow wrapped around its slopes. Mount Hermon, commonly known as Jabal el Sheikh, rises majesti-cally from the Beqaa plain, its heavy white beard a testament to its history.

We stop at one of the famous cedars, the 2,000-year-old Sheikha[37], where a frisky beagle pup joins us for a group picture.

Trees in the reserve are of varying ages, an indication of the different stages in the reforestation project. We come to a hillside with young saplings. Each has a small flag with a name on it. It is a poignant memorial to the soldiers who lost their lives at the battle of Nahr el Bared in 2007, far more meaningful than any statue or monument could ever be. We follow Chamoun on a small detour from the trail where he proudly shows us his "adopted" tree.

By 4 p.m., we reach the Barouk entrance of the reserve, where we will end our hike. I buy a case of cedar honey that is reputed to have unique properties that boost the immune system. It is the product of the Rural Development Program of the Chouf Biosphere Reserve, an initiative that aims to conserve and develop local foods.

Hospitality and generosity come naturally to our hosts, Ziad and Mirna Boustany. Mirna, a librarian, loves to cook and enjoys hosting the hikers that come through here. We are treated to a delicious meal of *adas bi hamod, burghol bi dfeen, baba ghannouj* (Marco's favorite), garden salad and of course Lebanese wine.

Opposite:
> VIEW OF MOUNT HERMON FROM BAROUK
> HANA AND MICHEL MOUFAREGE
Below:
> WOLF PRINT?
> APPROACHING THE CEDAR FOREST
> *ANEMONE BLANDA* SCHOTT AND KY

At the end of dinner, Sheikh Toufic Abu Alwan, from the village of Barouk arrives, to be interviewed by Marco. Born in Chile, he returned to Lebanon in the 60s to re-establish himself in his father's beloved hometown. He has many insights and opinions on rural issues and believes that Lebanon's centralized government is the source of most of the problems rural towns and villages face today. Inadequate health care, schooling, infrastructure, water and electricity are all a result of this "centralization."

It's time for my nightly journal entry, and I reach into the usual spot in my bag but the diary isn't there. I panic and then remember that I left one bag on the bus, which, Sultan tells me, is parked half a kilometer away. He walks with me in the dark narrow streets.

First we hear it coming and then we are practically blinded by the high beam of a speeding car coming right at us. We plaster ourselves against the wall as it zooms past. What the...? How can one manage to pick up that much speed on such narrow streets? It is either sheer lunacy or sheer drunkenness. We both say *'hamdillah al salameh* [38] and continue up to the bus as our racing heart rates normalize.

Diary found, we are walking back to the guesthouse when the maniac driver, finding us an amusing game, tries a second run. This time, our reflexes are up to the task and we hurriedly jump onto a convenient wall as he whizzes by.

------------------------

[36] Michel helped ECODIT delineate the path of the LMT, building on his vast experience and repertoire of hiking trails.
[37] A title accorded to women of high social standing.
[38] Thank God for your safety.

"As you sit on the hillside, or lie prone under the trees of the forest, or sprawl wet-legged by a mountain stream, the great door that does not look like a door, opens"

STEPHEN GRAHAM, *The Gentle Art of Tramping*

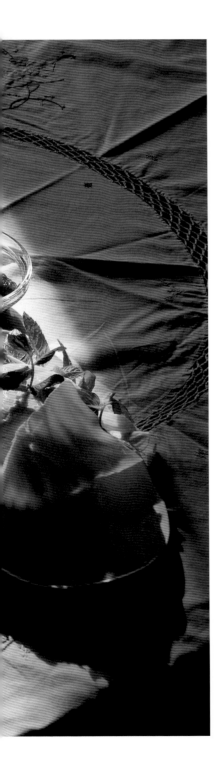

البـاروك إلى معاصر الشوف

# Barouk to Maasser El shouf

## Day 22

The Boustany's have prepared a beautiful breakfast, which, amid the soft rays of the morning sun, becomes the subject of a photo shoot for our hiking paparazzi.

This part of the Barouk reserve is said to have the highest concentration of 1,000-year-old cedars. I ask the ranger if he is annoyed by the random graffiti on many of the trees. He gives me a wry smile and says, "These trees will still be here long after the hands that carved these letters are buried in the dirt." One of my favorites is the Lamartine Cedar, named after Alphonse de Lamartine, the French Romantic poet who is said to have spent many reflective moments here while on his travels. Its massive canopy is so dense that even in the dead of winter, with meter-high snowdrifts, the area underneath remains dry and 40 people can easily sit beneath its boughs.

Norbert gets a mysterious text message from a friend; something about looking up into the branches of the Lamartine tree and "seeing Jesus." (Oddly enough, at the same spot we meet a missionary family from Texas.)

Previous pages:
> MIRNA AND ZIAD BOUSTANY'S BREAKFAST SPREAD
Below:
> ROCKY HILLSIDE BETWEEN THE BAROUK AND
MAASSER FORESTS
> A SPLASH OF YELLOW

Maurizio and Norbert climb the huge boulders around the tree
to get a better view of the surrounding area. Then Norbert
calls out to me and points to the rocks behind. It's a mouse. I
sit and wait for it. It comes out from a long crack in the rock. It
darts up the rock and returns with some blades of grass. The
industrious creature does this several times with a profound
sense of purpose. It is very round, so we figure it must be
pregnant and busy nesting. In fact, this is a great spot for an
expectant mother, with its steady supply of crumbs and tidbits.
She has big brown eyes, and we name her Sophia after the
Italian actress Sophia Loren.

Wild boars are quite common in the area. Our guide says he
saw a mother and her piglets here the day before. We can see
where they have plowed through the undergrowth. Even
though it is good for the soil, it sometimes disrupts the delicate saplings.

Close to the Maasser entrance stands the largest Cedar in the
forest. The eight of us hold hands around it and can barely en-
circle its massive 3,000-year-old trunk.

The long descent to the village of Maasser el Shouf begins in
the reserve. Soon the trees clear and the trail becomes rocky
with a scattering of junipers and oaks. Toward the bottom, the
trail disappears into the brush and we have to do some serious
bushwhacking[39]. At times the brush is so dense that we are
forced to scoot on our behinds or 'butt walk.' Poor Marco and
Maurizio decided to wear shorts.

> *LINUM PUBESCENS* BANKS AND SOL
> PATCHES OF SUNLIGHT IN THE CEDAR FOREST

As soon as we arrive at the town square, a shopkeeper summons us over. He is already setting up his "café trottoire," excited at the prospect of potential customers. Shamil Azzam's emporium sells an eclectic range of items: fireworks, hiking boots, herbal remedies, candy, beer and cigarettes. Meanwhile, his "café" offers grilled meat, sandwiches and even a hookah pipe, or *narguileh*.

"A sensitive plant in a garden grew,
And the young winds fed it with silver dew,
And it opened its fan-like leaves to the light,
and closed them beneath the kisses of night"

PERCY BYSSHE SHELLEY, *The Sensitive Plant*

معاصر الشوف إلى نيحا
# Maasser el shouf to Niha
## Day 23

Maurizio has been trying all morning to dry his socks. He finally has success using the Auberge's hair dryer.

We have a treat today. Not one, but two very special guides will be with us. Marwan Khodr, from Baakline, is an expert on wild vegetation, and is a self-taught guitarist who often brings his guitar into the mountains. He is a sensitive, serene soul who, corny as it sounds, exudes positive energy. He grows and presses his own olives, and is commonly known as Baba Bi'a, Father Nature.

Nazih Baz is from Baadarane. Following in his father's footsteps, he is an authority on Arab and herbal medicine, who studied in Russia. He also runs a *nol* weaving workshop. *Nol* is an almost extinct form of traditional Lebanese loom weaving, and some of his creations have won international awards.

The mountains are rounder and softer today. The fields are full of wildflowers, nodding wonders almost beyond counting. It has been over three weeks now and I am astounded that I am still discovering new species.

We pause by a patch of delicate amethyst-colored blooms. Wild orchids! I had no idea that wild orchids grew in Lebanon, let alone that there are 60 kinds, five of which are unique to Lebanon and are found between 500-1400 meters. Marwan tells me that the Arabic name for orchids is *sahlab*, the same name as the traditional breakfast drink, which is made from the bulb of the orchid plant.

After crossing a small brook, Marwan asks us to stop and listen for a moment. Silence. He draws our attention to how rarely in our modern, fast-paced lives we can hear "silence," that we seldom take the time to pause and listen to the sounds of nature.

We ascend along eroded sand hills striated in a spectrum of amber, copper and deep violet. At the top, we reach a flat saddle of land between two mountains, a meadow sprinkled with dainty florets. Lise-Lotte and Norbert have a *Sound of Music* moment, very apt, considering Norbert's Austrian lineage. Up ahead stands Niha Mountain with the white shrine of Nabi

Below:
> THE ORCHIDS AND US
> *ONOSMA FRUTESCENS* LAM.
Opposite:
> *ORCHIS ITALICA* POIRET
> IMPRESSIONIST INSPIRATION
> CAN YOU SPOT THE WHITE GOAT?

Ayoub, or Job, just visible near the peak. It is a perfect day: clear skies, balmy temperature, refreshing gentle breezes and the musical chatter of Italians.

The approach to the village of Niha is along a water canal that contours the side of the valley. The vegetation is rich and dense and below there are several farms and orchards. In one of the enclosures we see a large herd of jet black baby goats and I spot amongst them a single white one. The white goat of the family, perhaps.

At the town square, Norbert notices a very dignified Druze sheikh sitting on his front porch, his white moustache perfectly groomed. Under a black leather jacket he is wearing an embroidered vest and cummerbund, and of course the traditional *sherwal*. Druze villagers, especially the veiled women, do not like to

have their picture taken. Happily, it turns out that Izzat Arnous is friendly and cooperative and Norbert returns a happy man.

Our group has grown far beyond what we initially planned, pushing the capacity of the small guesthouse in Niha to its limit. My friend, Charlotte, joins us today and is a good sport about the "cozy" quarters. Having trekked in Nepal, she is used to less than perfect sleeping arrangements. The rest of the 15 weekend hikers are staying at a guesthouse in a neighboring town. Even though I am glad at all the attention the walk is receiving, I find myself selfishly resenting the intrusion on our harmonious little group. Norbert the matchmaker, on the other hand, is looking forward to interviewing prospective brides for Padre and Marathon Man.

*"Everybody needs beauty as well as bread, places to play in and pray in, where nature may heal and give strength to body and soul"*

JOHN MUIR

نيحا إلى جزين
# Niha to Jezzine
Day 24

The sun shining, we wait at the
entrance of the Mershad guesthouse for the rest of the hikers
to be dropped off. Joseph[40] and I take the opportunity to catch
up. He flew in from the US to hike the last week with us. The
LMT is Joseph's brainchild, a vision that through dedication
and hard work is now a reality.

A short walk to the edge of town and we are at the base of
Niha Mountain and an arduous 300m climb to the Nabi Ayoub
shrine looms ahead. Some of the newcomers soon fall behind.
This is not what they expected their stroll in the woods to be,
and after the first hundred meters they are gasping for air. A
couple decides to turn back and Lise-Lotte makes sure they
make it down safely. Early on, Maurizio and Marco decided to
teach me one Italian phrase a day. Today it's *una brisa fresca* (a
cold breeze), or is it *una bira fresca* (a cold beer)?

A large white stone building with an inner courtyard, the Nabi
Ayoub shrine is also a retreat for Druze elders and sheikhs. The
caretaker, Adel Boukarroum, meets us at the entrance and briefs
us on how we should behave while visiting the shrine – no food
or drink is one of the rules. The spacious terrace overlooks a

sweeping panorama of mountains and villages. There is one particularly interesting hillside with strata twisted by geological upheaval called "synclines."

We gather around in the generous shade of an old Oriental Arbutus berry tree. Adel tells us that Job's tomb is actually in Salalah, Oman. Job is mentioned in both the Old Testament and the Koran and the shrine marks the sacred spot of his miraculous healing. The story goes that Job, afflicted by a horrible flesh-eating disease, retreated for several years to this secluded hillside as a hermit. He never lost faith and, while lying in the shade of a large tree on the brink of death, a spring of water suddenly gushed out of the rock, its healing waters completely curing him. It is from this that the saying *saber Ayoub*, or the patience of Job, comes. His was a message of peace, love and healing and the spot is now a place of pilgrimage for afflicted people of all faiths.

Mr. Boukarroum goes on to explain the symbolism behind the Druze flag, in which the five pointed star represents the five senses, while the five colors – green, red, yellow, blue and

white – the five cosmic principles of the Mind (Wisdom), the Word (Truth), Self (the Soul), the Past (Reincarnation) and the Future (Judgment Day).

The trail to the Niha fortress contours the mountain over rolling hills and spring fields. The colossal cliff face towers high above the Bisri Valley. The rock castle, also known as Shqif Tyron, is part natural, part man-made. The cave-fortress consists of interlocking chambers and seven deep wells, three of which still have water. It was occupied by the Crusaders from 1165 to 1260 and is said to also have been the hiding place of Emir Fakhreddine II when he fled the Ottomans in 1635. He was later be captured and hanged in Jezzine. The roped path to the lofty cave is not for the faint hearted, with sheer cliffs dropping 400m into the valley. But it is worth it.

We come upon an abandoned farm, its fields fallow. Nazih explains that this is a common sight, as many small, family-owned farms have been unable to compete. We then traverse a broad valley with wonderfully gnarled delb trees on an islet in the river.

It is a short hike today, only 13km, but we don't get to Jezzine till 4 p.m. The pace is always slower with a large group as one has to make more stops. The last stretch to the town is a steep downhill on a paved road, but we have a lovely view of Jezzine

Previous pages:
> SYNCLINES, TWISTED STRATA IN THE NIHA AREA
Opposite:
> RIVER IN THE AZZIBE VALLEY
Below:
> GRIBBITT!

with its red-roofed houses and famous waterfall. It is much larger than I had imagined.

The first thing on my mind after checking in at the family run hotel is a hot shower. No such luck in our room, even after 30 minutes of well-meaning and dare I say, comedic, attempts by the whole family to remedy the problem. Bassem braves the cold water while I decide to sit on the bed and sulk.

In the lobby, the rest of the team revel in their squeaky cleanness. This only makes me grumpier. Lise-Lotte is rooming with Carrots[41] tonight. She quickly picks up on my crankiness and invites me to take a shower in their room after dinner hosted by the municipality at Shlouf, one of the two restaurants perched on the waterfall.

The Italians enjoy the *mezze,* especially the *kibbe nayeh*, and wash it down with *arak*. We have all lost weight considerably since leaving Qbaiyat, and this gives us free license to eat anything and everything we like, or as Norbert puts it, "We can eat like *hayawan.[42]*"

The big news tonight is that Maxime Chaya[43] has reached the North Pole. Everyone toasts and cheers. I leave them early and shower. By the time Bassem returns, I am in a better mood.

------------------------

[40] Joseph Karam is President and owner of ECODIT, the environmental and development consulting firm that conceived, designed and implemented the LMT project (2006-2008).
[41] Marie Chedid, a regular weekender, known for generously bringing carrots on the trail.
[42] Animal.
[43] The first Lebanese (and Arab) to complete "The Three Poles" (North Pole, South Pole, and Mt. Everest) as well as the world's seven highest summits.

*The South*

*"I perhaps owe having become a painter to flowers"*

CLAUDE MONET

جزين إلى عيتنيت
## Jezzine to Aitanit
### Day 25

We now number 43 and finding transport up to the trailhead is not easy.

Jezzine marks the beginning of the southern portion of the LMT and with it security issues. Two "hikers" from Hezbollah[44] were supposed to be joining us but couldn't make it. We will be hiking unescorted.

We pick up our lunches from a *dekkanneh* in the town square and our ride to the trailhead, an open-bed truck, arrives. I look at Padre with an are-you-kidding-me look, but he just smiles and motions me to climb on board. We pile in like sheep. The rollercoaster ride up the steep winding road is both funny and scary. Holding on for dear life through jolts and jerks while convulsing with laughter seems only to fuel the hilarity of the situation. I can only imagine what the sheep and goats grazing on the hillside are thinking.

It is a gradual but steady ascent up the Azzibe Valley to the pass on Jabal Niha. The riverbed, smoothed and polished by time, cradles several crystal clear pools and ponds interconnected by waterfalls and burbling brooks. Music to Marwan

Khodr's ears. He and Lise-Lotte have purposely fallen behind to escape the constant chatter of our enlarged group.

Leaving the valley, we head on through idyllic, rolling meadows of knee-deep grass and wildflowers. A canvas of fragrant pastel blooms. A crisp breeze and swirling puffy white clouds give us breaks from the bright sun. One particular hillside is so densely carpeted in flowers, it is a shame that we have to trudge through leaving a flattened winding trail in our wake.

The landscape then takes on a dramatic change of character with solitary windswept oaks, striking against a backdrop of sun-bleached rocks. Nizar[45] tells me these oaks are native to Lebanon, but that most are found only on this mountain. There is a wide dirt road running along the ridgeline, created before 2000 by the occupying Israeli forces. There are also several abandoned bunkers. One shack seems to be still in use, as the more inquisitive hikers discover a bag with fresh bread inside. Padre gets a bit nervous and asks them to rejoin the group.

There are many dolines or basins here. They are common to high lying areas and a result of snowmelt and a source of recharging and drainage for underground aquifers. We take refuge from the fierce winds in a large doline.

> DOLINE, BASIN AND THE LAST REMNANTS OF SNOW
> REACHING THE SANDSTONE PASS
> DESCENDING THE SANDSTONE GORGE

I look for Lise-Lotte and realize she and Nemir are missing. Padre waits for a while and goes back to look for them. Their familiar silhouettes soon appear on the ridge. Busy identifying flowers, they had fallen behind and were stopped and questioned by an armed member of Hezbollah. They are eager to tell us about their close encounter of the "Hizb" kind. "He must be very bored and lonely on that hilltop," Lise-Lotte remarks finally.

Progress along the craggy ridge is slow. The serrated rocks claim their share of cuts and torn clothing. We pass by el Sibeh (ladder) hill and soon get our first sweeping view of Lake Qaraoun and the Beqaa plain. The lake is a deep blue and the valley a patchwork of terracotta and emerald fields. I kneel down for a core team photo. The backpack makes me top-heavy, and as I try to get up, I lose my balance and start to fall backwards. Luckily, Padre has the reflexes of a Ninja and grabs me by the collar before I fall off the cliff!

We zigzag down the hillside toward the village of Aitanit. In the middle of a small oak forest, we stop at a landmark ancient oak. It is so huge there is a small pool of water in its trough-like trunk that's big enough to fit a person.

Clearing the forest we are welcomed by the fragrance of spartium bushes that cover the hillside all the way to the village. A man with jet black hair, a bushy beard and wild eyes is excitedly awaiting us on the outskirts of Aitanit. Maurice Habboush is a jack of all trades, he does odd jobs for the municipality, works on the family farm and does guide work. He wears his LMT t-shirt proudly.

Near the Saint George church, we stop at the spring of Ain el Dayaa to cool off and have a drink. Two old men come and chat with us. Nazih El-Rassi and Giryes Ayna have been friends

Below:
> NAZIH EL RASSI
> GIRYES AYNA
> STREAM IN AZZIBE EL EL FAWQA
Next pages:
> FIRST VIEW OF LAKE QARAOUN

their entire lives and are inseparable. Their twinkling eyes beam from faces wonderfully weathered by a lifetime of work in their apple and peach orchards. They tell us how much they miss their children, who have emigrated. Nazih reaches into his pocket and gives me a chocolate Easter egg.

Marie and her niece Nada have tea and cookies for us when we arrive at the guesthouse. Both are widows, and the guesthouse is an important source of income for them. Their candid and affable manner makes us feel at home right away. Aitanit's mayor, Assad Najm[46], drops in to visit and stays for dinner. It is refreshing to find somebody who recognizes the importance and potential of eco-tourism and is an active conservationist. The dinner spread is so packed with assorted dishes, that there is hardly an empty spot on the table. It seems we won't go hungry at Nada's.

------------------------

[44] Lebanese political party with a strong support base in South Lebanon.
[45] Nizar Hani was a member of the LMT Project team; he is also an expert on Lebanon's flora.
[46] Assad Najm is a founding member of the LMT Association.

"Where are the Doughnuts?"

عيتنيت

# Aitanit - Rest day
## Day 26

When I awake, the room is lit with a soft morning glow. Everyone is still asleep, even Lise-Lotte. I look out to a serene silvery lake and towering mountains enshrouded in a delicate lingering haze. Putting on a jacket over my long johns, I slip on my sneakers and cross the street to take a picture of this precious pre-dawn moment.

Padre and the four *ajeneb* leave early to get the military passes they will need for the remainder of the trip to Marjyaaoun. The rest of us laze around and catch up on errands and work. Joseph is eager to visit the new state-of-the-art water treatment plant at the foot of the Qaraoun dam. Padre returns a few hours later, mission accomplished and everybody heads out for the tour.

Norbert, Maurizio and I decide to stay behind and enjoy the sunny terrace overlooking the lake. Maurizio tells us about his business in Como, Italy. He leads hiking trips in Italy and abroad and makes posters of photographs from these trips. He also has a small awning business, which gives him access to celebrity homes on the lake, including George Clooney's.

Norbert tells us about covering wars to boat shows. He is plotting to play cupid with Chamoun and Marie's young helper, the sweet Berthe.

Nada has planned a barbecue lunch at a picnic spot known only to locals. The minivan takes us to Ain el Dib, just outside of Aitanit. The hillside of soft hued wild flowers is bespeckled with scarlet poppies. There is a long picnic table in the shade of a large walnut tree with a sweeping vista of the lake below and Mount Hermon, also known as Jabal el Sheikh, in the distance. Rising majestically from the plain, not a wisp of cloud obscures its summit.

The gushing water from the spring is channeled into canals that go around the picnic area, access to which is controlled by the municipality. The caretaker, Nuhad Rizk, welcomes us, her silvery-cropped hair framing a tanned face and sparkling eyes. She has lived in Aitanit all her life and is employed by the municipality to do odd jobs, including maintaining this site.

We take turns fanning the coals and turning the skewers. The homemade *arak* chills in the ice-cold water. Marco climbs up the tree with a bottle of beer.  When I ask him why, he explains that this is the smoking section. He has been with us for six days and I had no idea he smokes. With a bit of prompting from Joseph, Maurice breaks into a spontaneous *zajal*. I am astounded by his witty improvisations about our group, the trail and nature. After much prompting, Marco and Maurizio sing a popular Italian country song. It sounds so melodious and romantic. I ask them what it is about. "Oh, the village prostitute," replies Maurizio.

Padre and I head back to the house while the rest go for a boat ride. It sounds like fun, but I stay behind because I know I'll get cold. Nada and Marie are already back in the kitchen cooking up a storm, even though we can't even think of food. She just loves to feed people.

The boating party returns windblown and mellow, and they all retire to their rooms till dinnertime. We don't have the heart to tell Nada that we don't want to eat, so we sit around the table while the family hovers about us. Marie's seven-foot son Mansour joins us. He is fair, has blue eyes and looks like a New York cop. "Where are the doughnuts?" Norbert asks.

"The sun, with all those planets revolving around it and dependent on it, can still ripen a bunch of grapes as if it had nothing else in the universe to do"

GALILEO GALILEI

عيتنيت إلى راشيا
# Aitanit to Rachaiya
## Day 27

Nada and her family smother us in hugs before we leave to hike down to the lake shore and cross the dam.

A ferocious looking but friendly watchdog guards the spring at Ain el Dayaa, where we fill our water bottles and continue down, weaving through immaculately maintained almond and olive orchards. The field on the waterfront is strewn with gray and cream-colored flint rocks. This is where Maurice's duty ends, and where, Mahdi, our new guide from Rachaiya, takes over. From the dam, the Litani River continues its course southward. To the south is the newly inaugurated water treatment plant and on the mountainside to the east the town of Qaraoun.

A farm track road takes us by a sheep shearing compound, where a family of gypsies is busy sorting and shearing the flock. Being Bedouins, they have no official papers, yet they travel here every spring from Homs in central Syria. The children, charged with the task of herding the sheep, use plastic tubes to smack the unruly ones into line. It probably looks and sounds a lot more painful than it actually is.

The whole family has broad cheerful smiles and their colorful gypsy clothes reflect this vivacity. I notice a stunningly beautiful young girl standing by the paddock gate. At 15, Samar is the eldest child, and both Maurizio and Norbert are delighted when she allows them to take her photo.

We traverse a field in shoulder-high grass and an abundance of purple thistles. At the hilltop village of Majdel Balhis, we meet Mohammad Bou Leif standing by his pick-up truck. He is a goat trader from Rachaiya el Wadi and spring is a busy period for him.

The path continues over rolling hills till we reach a hidden valley of vineyards and orchards, which we cross following a country lane between two neatly planted vineyards. Joseph says these are some of the best table grapes in Lebanon.

The village of Kawkaba Bou Arab sits atop a large butte[47] and we end our steep and rigorous uphill at the shrine of Sheikh Fadel, where we cool off in the shade of ancient oaks.

The sleepy town awakens with our arrival. A shopkeeper opens her *dekkaneh* for us to buy cold drinks and goodies. A group of young men are gathered outside. All are talking on their cell phones and wearing gaudy fake Armani-esque buckles on their belts.

The machismo doesn't stop there. Soon we hear a revving engine and screeching tires, noises that herald the arrival of a souped-up BMW of a vintage favored by many young Lebanese men – antennas sticking out like a startled porcupine,

Previous pages:
> ON THE SHORE OF LAKE QARAOUN
> *AINSWORTHIA CORDATA* (L.F.) BOISS.
Opposite:
> STOPPING TO SMELL THE FLOWERS
Below:
> MOHAMMAD BOU LTEIF, A GOAT TRADER FROM
RACHAIYA EL WADI
> PATCHWORK FARM
Next pages:
> ARQOUB AT THE FOOTHILLS OF MOUNT HERMON

large doses of chrome and a throbbing stereo that could rival the village generator. Another even flashier "car" appears and we are quite flattered that our presence merits such a welcoming committee. The episode ends with no injuries due more to the dexterity and quick reflexes of the pedestrians, rather than the drivers' skills.

Our 24km trek ends with an arduous 300m climb to Rachaiya and its famous "Independence" castle, which sits on a wooded bluff overlooking the town[48]. We are now on the foothills of Mount Hermon. We walk through the cobbled streets of the old souk, lined with traditional stone houses with red-tiled roofs and wooden shutters and doors, and where the silver and gold smiths are renowned.

It is 6:30 p.m. when we arrive at the guesthouse. The sun is just falling behind the distant blue-gray ridges of the Chouf Mountains, draining the color from the valley below.

------------------------

[47] An isolated hill or mountain rising abruptly above the surrounding land.
[48] The historic fortification was built on the site of a medieval watchtower dating back to the 14th century. The French used the castle to imprison political activists working for Lebanon's independence in 1943.

"strange people are those who hike
Trekkers, ramblers, call them what you like
All are under her charm, under Nature's spell
Marveling at things small as a nutshell
A walking stick at hand and a backpack
All share one passion, all stroll the mountain track"

MICHEL MOUFAREGE

راشيا إلى حاصبيا
# Rachaiya to Hasbaiya
## Day 28

Our host, Kamal, takes us to the roof terrace for a view of Rachaiya. Contemplating this pictur-esque town with its red roofs, cobbled streets and greenery, I imagine a time when all Lebanese villages were like this – a time before the intrusion of billboards and high-rises crept into the rural idyll.

As we head out of the town, we receive countless invitations to coffee and breakfast. It would have been nice to spend more time here, but the trail beckons.

We will be skirting the foothills of Mount Hermon for most of the day. Rachaiya is one of the starting points for hikes to the 2,814m summit, Lebanon's second highest peak (the eastern face of the mountain lies in Syria while the southern side is in Israel). Mount Hermon is of significant biblical importance. It is where Jesus told the apostles he would go to Jerusalem to die and be resurrected. All very dramatic! At the summit, there is a Canaanite temple erected for pagan sun worship.

We encounter two elderly couples working in the fields. The men are friendly, chatting and joking with us, but the veiled

Previous pages:
> PASSING NEAR EL FAQAA HAMLET
Opposite:
> EL FAQAA HAMLET
Below:
> FARMER FROM AIN ATA
> CHAMOUN GIVES A LADY A HELPING HAND
> RACHAIYA ROOFTOPS

women are camera shy. Chamoun gives one of the ladies a hand with the hoe. Walking by a wire fence, I stop in my tracks before a jaw-dropping tableau: a sun-dappled orchard exploding in bloom with a carpet of lilac, white and yellow blossoms, against the backdrop of the mountain laced with white snowfields.

We pass by an unmanned army checkpoint. So far no one has checked the *ajnabis'* military passes and Padre wonders why he went to all the trouble of getting them. By noon we are getting hungry and weary, but our guide, Mahdi, has a special lunch spot in mind. "Just a little further," he says.
It is worth it. A grove of old oak trees covers the entire hillside. We settle down in their generous shade, cushioned by a

Previous pages:
> AIN TINTA AREA
> GRAZING ON THE FOOTHILLS OF MOUNT HERMON
Below:
> ABOU HADI FROM RACHAIYA EL WADI
Opposite:
> OAK GROVE NEAR AIN ATA

ground cover of delicately scented flowers. I look around at my friends and I notice the physical changes. We are all leaner and stronger. But the most remarkable change is that we truly seem to have shed wrinkles! Our worries and stresses reduced to the basic needs of food, water and sleep. I haven't used my credit card for a whole month!

The trail becomes steeper and rockier. Some of the group make a small detour to check out the cave of Ain Tinta, where bats have deposited a thick and stinky layer of drop-pings at the entrance, no doubt to deter visitors! Today is an-other 24km walk. On days like this, when the rocky downhills are taking their toll on my already swollen feet and my knees are beginning to protest, I try to maintain a slow pace but take very few breaks.

Soon, we see the town of Hasbaiya nestled between the wooded hills. We bushwhack through olive and fig groves until we reach the paved road leading to the town square and the Chehabi Castle. People call out to us from their patios "hawwil"⁴⁹.

Opposite:
> PINE FOREST NEAR AIN ATA
Below:
> WHAT GOES UP MUST COME DOWN
> *ACANTHUS SYRACUS* BOISS
Next pages:
> APPLE ORCHARD WITH MOUNT HERMON IN
THE BACKGROUND

Munzer Chehab, whose family is descended from nobility,
meets us in the town square and takes us to the inner courtyard of the castle. Crusaders built a watchtower on the site of
a Roman temple and the palace was built on top of the watchtower ruins. More intriguing layers of history. The castle is pri-
vately owned and Munzer's family occupies a small portion of
the 65-room property.

Parched and sore, we are eager to get to the guesthouse, which
is run by the youth organization SOIL (Save Our Inherited Land).

Later that night, I become aware of a sinking feeling in my
stomach, and beneath the usual joking and teasing there is an
air of wistfulness. It is our last night together in the mountains.
Our adventure is almost over.

------------------------

49 "Make a detour." An invitation to come visit.

"Two roads diverged in a wood, and I—
I took the one less traveled by,
And that has made all the difference"

ROBERT FROST, *The Road Not Taken*

حاصبيا إلى مرجعيون

# Hasbaiya to Marjaayoun
## Day 29

**15.6.** That's how many kilometers remain of our 440km journey. Wim had calculated our cumulative uphill and downhill elevation gain: 20,000m. That is two and a half times the height of Mount Everest. It is a bit hard to believe, but then again the past 30 days have gone by incredibly fast. Our morning preparations have become second nature by now and we get ready as normal despite the significance of the day.

At the edge of the town we stop to visit the church of Mar Giryes. Outside the church is a toppled statue of St. George on his horse broken in two. In the large slab of white rock are what look like large hoof prints. Legend has it that they are the prints of St. George's horse.

We head down agricultural footpaths towards the oak forests of Hima[50] Hasbaiya, woodland so dense it is virtually impenetrable. We skirt the perimeter of the forest through shoulder high grass, flowers and thistle. The trail clears as we head out along the Hasbani River valley. The thick vegetation is replaced by rolling hills of olive groves. The thick trunked trees,

Previous pages:
> CROSSING THE HASBANI RIVER
> HASBANI VALLEY
Opposite:
> HIMA IBL ES SAQI
> NARROW-LEAVED VIPER'S BUGLOSS, *ECHIUM
ANGUSTFOLIUM*
> INSIDE HIMA IBL ES SAQI
Below:
> *CISTUS CRETICUS*

many over a thousand years old, are testimony to ancient crops dating back to biblical times.

The river crossing is tricky. The water level is so high that it flows over the walls of the small dam, and we are forced to leap from one water-covered pillar to the next. Apart from getting a muddy backside, I make it across.

We follow the riverbank till we reach Souk el Khan. The restored market is home to the Tuesday market and was originally built by Ali, son of Emir Fakhreddine el Maani. The neighboring caravanserai was on the ancient Silk Route. It is quite impressive despite undergoing poorly executed restoration.

Hima Ibl es Saqi has been partially reforested by the French government and is protected by the local community. An important area for bird watching, I find it ironic to happen upon two dead storks, victims of "hunting."

The main street in Ibl es Saqi is lined with a myriad of stores catering to UNIFIL soldiers, the area's main customers. We stop and chat with a group from a French contingent standing around an armored personnel carrier. Inquisitive about our journey, Padre shows them some of the topographical maps of the LMT. They are very impressed with the quality.

Then we get the news: we are informed that we cannot hike the rest of the way to Marjaayoun for "security reasons." Disappointed – our trek has given us a sense of entitlement to finish what we started on foot – we grudgingly get on the bus and Sultan drives us to the foot of the hill leading up to Marjaayoun and drops us off.

Our pace is quickened by the urgency of knowing we are on the home stretch. Suddenly, we find ourselves in the town square, surrounded by press, cameras and friends. I had envisioned the last leg differently: walking towards Marjaayoun

with the excitement building up to a peak. Instead I am taken, almost by surprise as it dawns on me that I have just taken my last
step. It takes a minute to sink in. We've done it! We have just
walked the length (and width) of the country. Amidst all the
hugs, I see that some of the guys are a also bit misty-eyed.

The press conference is held in front of the beautifully renovated municipality building. After the usual speeches by vari-
ous officials, we are each asked about our personal
impressions of the thru-walk. It's all a bit of a blur, but I say
something about how this was a journey of discovery and sur-
prising diversity on every level; that every town and village we
stayed in was different and special and that our hosts, from
different confessions all shared one quality: a natural capacity

for warm and generous hospitality. I think of it as a unifying string that runs down the backbone of the country. I am relieved when Maurizio reassures me that I was coherent.

It is a bittersweet moment as we get on the bus for the last time. The euphoria of accomplishment and the thrill of having taken part in something never done before is mixed with a sense of anti-climax and melancholy. I will miss my team and the fellowship of the trail: Lise-Lotte's no-nonsense wisdom and comforting companionship; Padre's leadership and dedication to conservancy; Norbert's humor and passion for the mountains; the reticent, yet easy-going Wim; and last but not least the eccentric Chamoun, a man on a mission to preserve the Lebanese mountains.

And lastly, the trail that was our home for a month, one that not only challenged and tested us, but also rewarded us generously, and often unexpectedly. It had been a journey of a million steps filled with wonder, serendipity and beauty.

Now I could go home.

------------------------

[50] An ancient form of community-based protected area, rooted in Arab societies.

Standing left to right:
> CHAMOUN, NORBERT, CHRISTIAN
Sitting left to right:
> WIM, LISE-LOTTE, HANA

# The team

> **Chamoun Mouannes (Marathon Man)** is a marathon runner and member of the Beirut Marathon Association. He has criss-crossed the country on foot covering over 4,000km with his trademark Lebanese flag sticking out of his backpack. His mission this trek was to get as many signatures possible on a petition to protect and preserve the LMT and its environs. Chamoun was also clearing the trails as we went. If ever anyone could make something this difficult seem easy, it was Chamoun!

> **Wim Balvert (Hollandi)** came all the way from, yes you guessed it, Holland to take part in this trek. He received the invitation a week before we began and, on the spur of the moment, decided to join us. He is an avid hiker, but this was his first time hiking in Lebanon. It takes a certain type of person decide to trek the entire length of a country at a week's notice.

> **Lise-Lotte Sulukjian (Sunshine)** moved to Lebanon in 1975 after falling in love with her future husband and his country and lived through the entire 75-90 Civil War. She is an experienced guide with Libantrek and has hiked much of the LMT many times. She also loves sailing her boat in the Mediterranean. Originally, Lise-Lotte was not slated to do the through walk but decided at the last minute to join us! It was really nice not being the only woman on the trip, and she was an absolute inspiration to trek with, which is why she was nicknamed Sunshine.

> **Christian Akhrass (Padre)** is the organizer and leader of the through walk. A member of the Lebanon Mountain Trail Assiocation (LMTA), he is an experienced mountain guide, environmental activist and member of the *Association Libanaise d'etudes Speleologiques* (ALES). He is a man with a strong passion for juniper trees, often referring to them as *habibti* (my love). Walking with Chris has raised my awareness of the environmental issues facing Lebanon's fauna and flora.

> **Norbert Schiller (Nimsawi)** was the photographer who helped me tell the story of this trek through his images. He has lived in the Middle East and Africa for over 20 years and has covered conflicts in Algeria, Iraq, Israel, the Palestinian territories, Sudan, Kurdistan and the Western Sahara. His books on Lebanon include: *Wines of Lebanon, Arak and Mezze: the Taste of Lebanon* and *Chateau Ksara: 150 Years of Winemaking*. His passion for Lebanon rivals, and often exceeds, that of many Lebanese.

# Glossary of Arabic terms

Transliteration of place names is according to the LMT guidebook. Fact checking, as well as captions and flower identification, has been corroborated by ECODIT and the LMTA

**A**
*Abu:* Father (of)
*Ajnabi (Ajeneb pl.):* Foreigner
*Ain:* Source or spring
*Arz:* Cedar
*Asfour (Asafir pl.):* Bird

**B**
*Baladi:* local
*Burghol bi dfeen:* A dish made with cracked wheat, meat, chick peas and onions

**D**
*Debs bi tahini:* Mixture of carob molasses with tahini, a sesame seed paste
*Deir:* Monastery or convent
*Dekkaneh:* small grocery store
*Diwan:* reception room or traditional Arabic sofa

**E**
*Emir:* Prince

**F**
*Fallah:* Farm worker
*Foul (pronounced fool):* Traditional breakfast dish of fava beans

**G**
*Giryes:* George

**H**
*Habibi (Habibti fem.):* My sweetheart
*Hosn:* Fortress

**I**
*Ibreeq:* Lebanese water jug
*Imm:* Mother (of)
*Inshallah:* God willing

**J**
*Jabal:* Mountain, Mount
*Jawz:* Walnut

**M**
*Maamoul:* Traditional sweet made from semolina, with a walnut, pistachio or date filling
*Mandaloun:* Traditional Lebanese arches
*Manousheh (manakeesh pl.):* Lebanese flat bread, typically made with thyme and olive oil
*Mar:* Saint
*Mezza:* Selection of dishes usually served as the first course in an Arabic meal

**N**
*Nabaa:* Spring
*Nabi:* Prophet
*Nahr:* River

**S**
*Saj:* Dome shaped baking plate used in preparing flat breads
*Salib:* Cross
*Soubhiyyeh:* Morning visit
*Souk:* Market

**T**
*Tahini:* Sesame seed emulsion
*Tallet:* Hilltop
*Teta:* Grandmother

**W**
*Wadi:* Valley

**Z**
*Zaatar:* Thyme, usually mixed with olive oil
*Zajal:* Oral, improvised poetry, sung, usually spontaneously, often in praise of those present

In memory of Abu Tareq